191 of 303

Also by Larry B. Massie

Michigan Memories (1994)
Birchbark Belles (1993)
Potawatomi Tears & Petticoat Pioneers
(1992)
The Romance of Michigan's Past (1991)
Pig Boats & River Hogs (1990)
Copper Trails & Iron Rails (1989)
Voyages Into Michigan's Past (1988)
Warm Friends & Wooden Shoes (1988)
From Frontier Folk to Factory Smoke
(1987)
    with Priscilla Massie
Walnut Pickles & Watermelon Cake (1990)
    with Peter Schmitt
Battle Creek: The Place Behind the
Product (1984)
Kalamazoo: The Place Behind the Product
(1981)

On the Road
to
Michigan's Past

Our Bark Canoe.

The road to Michigan's past is not without its hazards!

On the Road
to
Michigan's Past

by
Larry B. Massie

The Priscilla Press
Allegan Forest, Michigan
1995

Cover by Judi Miller Morris
Title Graphic by Devon Blackwood
Photographic Processing
 by Loren McKinstry

ISBN: Soft Cover   1-886167-03-6
      Hard Cover   1-886167-04-4

For Marguerite Miller and John Pahl, in appreciation for their tireless zeal in preserving, making available and promoting the heritage of the county that is my home.

Table of Contents

Preface

"Oh Come With Me
On a Magical Road
It'll Carry Us Backwards,
Through Time, I'm Told"

Some say that time is like a river, a continuum ever flowing onward with an energy all it own. I'm more inclined to see time as a road - a two way street. After all, roads are made by people and to me time is not a natural occurrence but a manmade measurement - a record of deeds and daring, or heroes and villains, of inventions and new ideas, of dreams realized and hopes unrequited, of sad war its tragedy and triumph, of civilizations' ebb and flow, and especially of books whose precious pages capture the past, awaiting only a reader to free golden days from time's fetters.

Come with me as a pilgrim on time's thoroughfare to a Michigan that once was. Forsake the honk and rush of truck ruled interstates for more sensible streets. Journey, instead, on narrow concrete stretches built for curved dash Oldsmobiles and Model T Fords. Beat out time to the rhythmic clip-clop of horse hooves, of spinning buggy wheels, of high stepping steeds and gay sleigh rides.

Let us travel in company with saddlebag doctors and snowshoe priests, with plaid-clad shanty boys en route to a winter hewing pine in the north woods, with Cornish copper miners keen to moil for red metal in the Keweenaw and with French explorers seeking the fabled water route to the Orient. Stroll with me as we thump along board sidewalks past Greek Revival and Italianate facades; and let us peer into dimly lit shop windows piled high with cast iron toys, kerosene lamps, ironstone china, Winchester rifles, horsehair blankets and fashions in crinoline and lace from days forever flown. Let us listen in on general store and barbershop gatherings to hear talk of hometown heroes and downtown dramas, of passenger pigeon nestings and glorious grayling fishing, of daring horse tamers and supernatural visions that launched health food empires, of pineland politics and railroad riches, of Civil War battles and County Seat Wars.

Board a stagecoach with me and fly along smooth plank roads. Plod with me alongside lumbering oxen pulling covered wagons heaped high with immigrant families, all their worldly possessions and hopes for a new life amid the big trees of Michigania. Let us wend our way along dusty country roads over-arched in leafy tunnels, tramp past overgrown cemeteries where sleep the pioneers, jog along voyageur's portage ways and thread mocassin beat Indian trails. And wearied from our travels let us cower closer to our wilderness campfire at night to hear tales of Potawatomi pluck and Ottawa lore of Chippewa Chiefs and Hiawatha's wooing as the mournful wail of wolves send shivers up your spines.

I hope you enjoy wandering along the road to Michigan's past as much as I have delighted in mapping out our itinerary.

Larry B. Massie
Allegan Forest, Michigan

Father Hennepin & the Voyage of the *Griffin*

The *Griffin* had just rounded Presque Isle Point, approximately halfway between present day Alpena and Rogers City, when a furious gale struck from the southwest. The helmsman, known only as Luc, managed to hold the little vessel in the face of the wind until morning when the increasing violence of the storm forced the crew to haul down the main yards and top mast and "let the ship drive at the mercy of the wind, knowing no place to run into to shelter ourselves." It was August 26, 1679, and the *Griffin*, the first ship to ply the water of lakes Erie, Huron and Michigan, was in desperate straits.

By noon the storm had intensified, heaving up great waves that flung the 45-60 ton vessel about as if it were a dinghy. With green water washing over the deck, the 53 men aboard retreated below where their commander, Robert Rene Cavelier, Sieur de La Salle, "notwithstanding he was a courageous man, began to fear, and told us we were undone; and therefore everybody fell upon his knees to say his prayers, and prepare himself for death." Everybody that is except the irreligious Luc. He, according to Father Louis Hennepin, a Recollect priest who recorded his experiences during the voyage of the *Griffin*, "did nothing all that while but curse and swear against M. La Salle, who, as he said, had brought him thither to make him perish in a nasty lake, and lose the glory he had acquired by his long and happy navigations on the ocean."

Despite Luc's imprecations, the wind abated somewhat and the crew managed to hoist some sail and avert disaster. The *Griffin* anchored in the shelter of East Moran Bay before St. Ignace the following day. Luc's tirade against his commander, however,

13

revealed a strong willed and irreverent personality which would ultimately prove the undoing of the expedition.

The building of the *Griffin*, La Salle's voyage of discovery and the mystery behind that ship's disappearance form one of the most fascinating chapters in early Michigan history. Hennepin's books comprise a major source for our knowledge of this topic. His first book, *A Description of Louisiana*, published in Paris in 1683, offers 32 pages relating to the *Griffin*. Unfortunately for the good friar's reputation, 21 of those pages were apparently plagiarized almost literally from the official record of the voyage communicated by La Salle to the French Minister of the Marine the previous year. In his second travel narrative, *A New Discovery of a Vast Country in America*, first published in Utrecht in 1697, Hennepin adds considerable details to the *Griffin* adventure, some of which do not agree with his earlier account. For example, his second book increases the size of the vessel from 45 to 60 tons but reduces the number of cannons aboard from seven to five.

The major problem with Hennepin's *New Discovery*, however, lies with his addition of a spurious voyage down the Mississippi to its mouth by himself, prior to that of La Salle, thus robbing his former patron of his most illustrious achievement. While La Salle, who by the time of the book's publication had been assassinated by his own mutinous men on the Brazos River in Texas, could not object to Hennepin's falsehoods, later historians such as the distinguished Milo Quaife have labeled the literary priest "a vain and boastful vagabond, treacherous, vengeful and dishonest."

Despite that rather serious caveat, Quaife and other reputable historians have used Hennepin's colorful accounts, buttressed by other contemporary French records reprinted in the 1870s in a six volume collection by Pierre Margry, as a primary source for the *Griffin* saga.

Born about 1640 in Ath, Belgium, Hennepin had early developed a passion to travel to unknown lands. Despite his priestly calling he enjoyed eavesdropping on sailors regaling tavern patrons with their tales of adventure. After serving as a chaplain in the war between France and Holland, Hennepin was delighted to be assigned to New France upon the request of its governor, Count Frontenac. La Salle was among the fellow passengers on the ship which carried Hennepin to Quebec in 1675 and the two seem to have struck up a friendship en route.

Three years later when La Salle, a protege of Frontenac, secured permission to embark on a three fold mission hoping to recoup his fortune - via a lucrative Lake Michigan fur trade, to discover a water route to the Gulf of Mexico, and construct a chain of forts from Canada southward that would insure French control over the continent's interior - he requested his friend Hennepin accompany the expedition.

La Salle established a shipyard above Niagara Falls, just west of the mouth of Cayuga Creek, where under the supervision of his trusted lieutenant Henri de Tonty, "the man with the iron hand," skilled carpenters constructed the *Griffin* during the winter and spring of 1679. Most of the resident Iroquois braves were away on the warpath to the west but some of those present sought to sabotage the construction of the ship. La Salle promised ten gold pieces to the chief ship builder as a bonus to speed up the work. Hennepin, who served as chaplain at the ship building camp, buoyed up the depressed spirits of the workers by exhorting them as to the glory and good of the mission.

Fearing an attack by the Indians, the ship builders launched the vessel's hull in May. After

Hennepin's 1697 publication included a print of the construction of the *Griffin* near Buffalo in 1679.

firing guns, singing the *Te Deum* and quaffing brandy in celebration, the party promptly took up residence in what had become a floating fort. Hennepin related that La Salle named the vessel the *Griffin* in honor of the mythological creatures which figured in Frontenac's coat of arms and that the prow of the ship was decorated with a carved griffin's head, but that is nowhere else corroborated. La Salle never referred to the vessel as the *Griffin* in his reports.

After several attempts to get the vessel up the strong current of the Niagara River, which Luc said could not be done, La Salle arrived with an extra anchor and additional rigging and the crew succeeded in sailing and towing the vessel from shore into Lake Erie on August 7, 1679. The *Griffin* enjoyed three days of smooth sailing to the mouth of the Detroit River. While passing up the river between Grosse Isle and Belle Isle, Hennepin found the future site of Detroit nearly akin to the Garden of Eden:

> The Country between those two Lakes is very well situated, and the Soil very fertile. The Banks of the Strait are vast Meadows, and the Prospect is terminated with some Hills covered with Vineyards, Trees bearing good Fruit, Groves, and Forests so well disposed, that one would think Nature alone could not have made, without the help of Art, so charming a Prospect. That Country is stocked with Stags, Wild-Goats, and Bears, which are good for Food, and not fierce as in other Counties; some think they are better than our Pork. Turkey Cocks and Swans are also very common; and our Men brought several other Beasts and Birds, whose Names are unknown to us but they are extraordinary relishing.
> The Forests are chiefly made up of Walnut trees Chestnut trees, Plum trees, and Pear trees, loaded with their own Fruit and Vines. There is also

abundance of Timber fit for building; so that those who shall be so happy as to inhabit that Nobel Country, cannot but remember with Gratitude those who have discovered the way, by venturing to sail upon an unknown Lake for above one hundred Leagues.

Continuing north, the explorers experienced some difficulty in sounding a passage through the St. Clair Flats, the lake being so named by Hennepin because that day marked the festival of Sainte Claire. Finally sailing out upon Lake Huron and continuing north along the Michigan coast, the *Griffin* encountered the savage gale which nearly brought an end to the journey. On August 27, the vessel cast anchor at St. Ignace, astonishing the resident Huron and Ottawa with a salute from its cannons. Those tribesmen, who were allied against the Iroquois, greeted the French visitors, crowding around the ship in more than 60 bark canoes to admire the European's "fine Wooden Canoe." La Salle visited the Ottawa village, finely dressed in a scarlet cloak with broad gold lace, and Hennepin celebrated mass there. They then toured the palisaded village of the Huron, who greeted them with a three round salute of all their muskets.

At the Straits La Salle discovered that a contingent of men he had sent ahead to trade with the Indians had deserted, absconding with a quantity of supplies to Sault Ste. Marie. He dispatched Tonty to the Sault after them. Owing to the lateness of the season, La Salle pushed on across Lac de Illinois (Lake Michigan) to Green Bay.

At a large village of Potawatomi on Washington Island La Salle encountered another group of his advance traders who had assembled a choice batch of furs. Although his men advised against it, La Salle, who, according to Hennepin, "never took any one's advice," loaded the *Griffin* with the furs and sent it back to Niagara Falls, manned by Luc and a crew of five. Luc's orders were to deliver his cargo, then to return to Michilimackinac for directions to a yet undetermined rendezvous point. Luc sailed from Washington Island on September 18 with a westerly wind, firing a cannon in salute as he departed. That would be the last La Salle or any other European ever saw of the *Griffin*. In his 1697 publication Hennepin described what the French explorer later learned concerning the loss of the vessel:

> The Ship came to an Anchor to the North of Lake of the *Illinois*, where she was seen by some Savages, who told us that they advised our Men to sail along the coast, and not towards the middle of the Lake because of the Sands that make the Navigation dangerous when there is any high Wind. Our Pilot, as I said before, was dissatisfied and would steer as he pleased without hearkening to the Advice of the Savages, who, generally speaking, have more Sense than the *Europeans* think at first: but the Ship was hardly a League from the coast, when it was tossed up by a violent Storm in such a manner, that our Men were never heard of since; and it is supposed that the Ship struck upon a Sand, and was there buried.

What curses the salty old seaman directed at La Salle as he went to his watery grave can only be imagined. But according to contemporary documents reprinted in Margry as cited by Buffalo historian O. H. Marshall in an 1879 article "a hatchway, a cabin door, the truck of a flag-staff, a piece of rope, a pack of spoiled beaver skins, two pair of linen breeches torn and spoiled with tar, were subsequently found and recognized as relics of the ill-fated ship."

19

Following the departure of the *Griffin* from Washington Island, La Salle and 14 of his men set out in four canoes to the south. Halfway from the island to the mainland, the same gale which presumably wrecked the *Griffin* nearly swamped La Salle's canoes. The explorers managed to take shelter in a small sandy bay where they waited five days for the storm to end then proceeded south along the west coast of Lake Michigan. After rounding the tip of the lake at the present site of Chicago, La Salle's party landed at the mouth of the St. Joseph River on November 1. While waiting for the return of Tonty and news of the *Griffin*, La Salle's men constructed Fort Miami atop a high bluff overlooking the river at present day St. Joseph, the first European outpost in the Lower Peninsula. Finally realizing that the *Griffin* was probably lost, La Salle and 30 of his men set out in eight canoes to continue their mission to the Mississippi River.

Thus ended Hennepin's narrative about the *Griffin*. While La Salle would not succeed in his goal of reaching the mouth of the Mississippi during that attempt, he would return. On April 9, 1682, at the Gulf of Mexico he would planted a cross bearing the Arms of France and claim for his king the entire Mississippi Valley.

Hennepin's two travel narratives and a third hastily prepared compilation he published in 1698, enjoyed great popularity, running through numerous French, Dutch, German, Italian, Spanish and English editions. Despite the rascally friar's plagiarism and prevarications his books did much to advertise the new western country throughout Europe and they first promoted the Lower Peninsula of Michigan.

Despite the periodic discovery of wreckage of ancient vessels, the exact fate and final resting place of the *Griffin* remain a tantalizing mystery.

Judgement at the Straits

The "trial of the century" had reached its climactic moment. The long wait was over. Now the judge, counselors, witnesses and crowd of spectators watched in hushed silence as the murder defendant inadvertantly confessed his guilt.

This sensational trial occurred not in a nationally televised Los Angeles courtroom in 1995 but in a log cabin on the remote Michigan frontier more than three centuries before. And while that California case would grip America's attention via sophisticated technology and forensic hoopla, the primitive court proceedings held beside the lapping waters of the Straits of Mackinac would result in a legal milestone - the introduction of European justice to a wilderness empire.

Our story begins earlier in the year, 1683, with the departure from Sault Ste. Marie of two fur traders laden with an ample stock of tobacco, gun powder, bales of cloth and other trade goods. Jacques Le Maire and Colin Berthat would never reach their destination, a post on the Keewenaw Peninsula not far from the ancient portage on Keewenaw Bay. Ambushed and killed by a party of Ottawa en route, their bodies were buried beneath piles of branches in a nearby swamp and their valuable cargo cached in several locations.

Unfortunately for the perpetrators, they failed to keep their crime a secret, secumbing to that time honored defect among criminals, the temptation to boast. One of the murderers, Folle Avione (Rice Man), arrived in the Sault in company with 15 Indian families who had fled from their Chequamenon Bay village in fear of an attack by their traditional enemies, the Sioux.

Despite widespread knowledge of his guilt, the

Rice Man thought himself safe given his many Chippewa companions who had declared "that they would not allow the French to redden the land of their fathers with the blood of their brothers." Against such overwhelming odds the dozen Frenchmen at the Sault felt themselves powerless to arrest the murderer.

That is where Daniel Greysolon, Sieur Duluth, (variously spelled Dulhuth or Du L'hut) enters the picture. Born in Saint-Germain-Laval, France, in 1639, as a teenager Duluth had chosen the profession of soldier, receiving a commission in the elite King's Guard. He had made two visits to New France, where several relatives lived, and shortly after participating in the bloody Battle of Seneff in 1674, he immigrated to Montreal.

In this strange unexplored new land Duluth became a courier de bois, and more than the usual connotation of the term, unlicensed Indian trader, he thirsted for knowledge of the fabled water route to the South Sea and the legendary copper mines in the unknown land to the west. He also adopted the role of diplomat, seeking to bring peace to the warring tribes so that the lucrative fur trade might continue unmolested.

With a crew of seven voyageurs Duluth struck out from Montreal in September, 1678, wintering in Sault Ste. Marie. There he won the support of the resident Saulteurs (a band of Chippewa). The following spring he and his voyageurs paddled to the head of Lake Superior where he conducted a peace treaty between the ancestral enemies, the Chippewa and the Sioux. Returning with the Sioux representatives to their village in Minnesota, near the upper Mississippi, Duluth hoisted the Royal *fleur de lis* and claimed the entire domain of the Sioux for the King of France. Other explorations and adventures followed in rapid succession, highlighted perhaps by his bold rescue in 1680 of Father Louis Hennepin held

Harper's magazine illustrator C.S. Reinhart sketched Duluth claiming the domain of the Sioux for his king.

23

captive by a band of 1,000 Sioux.

The year 1683 found Duluth commandant at Fort Michilimackinac at present day Mackinaw City. On October 24th a breathless courier arrived at the fort guarding the strategic Straits of Mackinac with news that the Rice Man, well known to Duluth as a suspect in the French traders' murder, was at the Sault. In company with six Frenchmen and a Jesuit missionary, Duluth embarked at dawn the next morning for the Sault. Three miles downstream from the rapids, Duluth landed. Dividing his party, half continued up the river while he and three companions traveled overland so as to surprise the culprit. At the Indian village near the rapids, Duluth boldly rushed in and arrested the Rice Man, placing him under constant guard.

In the meantime, Duluth had dispatched a trusted lieutenant, Jean Pere, to the Keweenaw country to arrest the others who had been implicated in the crime, an old Ottawa chief named Achiganaga and two of his sons. Following his seizure of the Rice Man, Duluth called the Indians present at the Sault into council, urging them not to protect those guilty of murdering Frenchmen lest they too be held accountable. During the ensuing repeated councils the Indians sought only to exculpate the Rice Man, blaming the deed solely on Achiganaga who they thought Pere would never be able to capture.

For three days those deliberations continued, without result whereupon Duluth left with his prisoner for Michilimackinac, "sustained by only twelve Frenchmen, to show a few seditious persons who boasted of taking the prisoner away from me, that the French did not fear them."

Thus the matter rested during the succeeding month as Duluth kept the Rice Man in custody at Fort Michilimackinac while daily came reports of the increasing numbers of allies Achiganaga was drawing to Keweenaw to protect his family. Those troubling reports, Duluth, wrote "placed me between hope and fear respecting the expedition which Pare had undertaken."

Suddenly at 10 o'clock on the evening of November 24, Pare arrived at Fort Michilimackinac, having traveled cross county through the woods on foot. Against overwhelming odds, he, in concert with 18 French traders wintering at Keweenaw, had succeeded in arresting Achiganaga and his sons. He had left them under guard some 12 miles west of the Sault. Early the next morning Pare left with additional men from the fort to retrieve his prisoners, arriving back at Michilimackinac later that afternoon. Duluth locked his prisoners in a room in his own house under strong guard.

The following day the trial began. Duluth gave notice to the various chiefs and elders in the Ottawa and Chippewa fortified villages clustered near Fort Michilimackinac to appear in council. He also notified the defendants that they could each select two relatives to act as their counsel during the trial. Duluth described the climax of the proceedings in a report to Joseph Antoine Le Febvre de La Barre, Governor General of New France :

> The council being assembled, I sent for Folle-Avione to be interrogated, and caused his answers to be written; and afterwards they were read to him, and inquiry made whether they were not, word for word, what he had said. He was then removed from the council under a safe guard. I used the same form with the two eldest sons of Achiganaga; and as Folle-Avoine had indirectly charged the father with being accessory to the murder, I sent for him, and also for Folle-Avoine, and bringing them into the council, confronted the four. Folle-Avoine and the two sons of Achiganaga accused each other of committing the

25

murder, without denying that they were participators in the crime. Achiganaga alone strongly maintained that he knew nothing of the the design of Folle-Avoine, nor of his children, and called on them to say if he had counselled them to kill the Frenchman. They answered "No!" This confrontation, which the savages did not expect, surprised them; and seeing the prisoners had convicted themselves of the murder, the chiefs said: "It is enough, you accuse yourselves; the French are masters of your bodies."

The guilt having been fully established in Duluth's mind, he called together other councils over the following days to offer the Indians the opportunity of dispensing justice their own way - to themselves execute the murderers. When those councils "ended only in reducing tobacco to ashes" Duluth told the chiefs that since they did not wish to decide he would take the responsibility.

Gathering together the entire body of French at the fort, the evidence from the trail was reviewed and then that jury voted. The verdict was unanimous - the Rice Man and Achiganaga's sons should die. Duluth decided on his own for leniency - since two Frenchmen had been killed only two of the guilty would have to atone with their lives. Accordingly, he pardoned the younger of Achiganaga's sons and then announced his decision to put the other two to death to the assembled chiefs, " a hard stroke to them all, for none had believed that I would dare undertake it."

In the midst of attempts of some of the chiefs to trade Iroquois captives for the lives of their tribesmen, Duluth terminated the council, telling the Indians that the result "was but the fruit of their own teaching. They had taught their youth that to kill a Frenchman was not an affair of much importance." Now they would learn otherwise.

The Jesuit fathers at the fort baptised the condemned Indians and an hour later, Duluth put himself "at the head of forty two Frenchmen, and in sight of more then four hundred savages, and within two hundred paces of their fort, I caused the two murderers to be shot" (varient translations of Duluth's report read that "he had their heads broken," a common form of military execution of the period being to have the culprit clubbed to death by a file of soldiers).

Whether it came about by bullet or rifle butt, the outcome was the same - the first recorded case of capital punishment in Michigan had been carried out. The harsh example apparently was successful, in the short run at least, in inspiring the desired effect of Indian respect for French law.

Over the succeeding 15 years Duluth would accomplish other notable exploits in the annals of New France and the Lake Superior country which honors his name in a Minnesota port city. In 1686 he established the short lived Fort St. Joseph at the present site of Port Huron. Duluth died in Montreal in 1710. One hundred and thirty six years later Michigan would become the first state to abolish capital punishment for murder.

The Sad Case of
Major Robert Rogers

The field of Ottawa, Potawatomi, Huron, and other Great Lakes tribesmen who had battled the British during the long and bloody French and Indian War gazed in silent awe as the *fleur de lis* emblazoned pennant sank slowly down the flagstaff. Then, as the Union Jack rose to flap over the palisades of Fort Pontchartrain, 700 Indian voices rose in a great prolonged shout. It was the afternoon of November 29, 1760, a day that marked the end of French control over the strategic post at the Straits of Detroit founded by Antoine Cadillac 59 years before.

With a force of 200 of his famed rangers and 75 additional troops Major Robert Rogers had journeyed to Detroit to accept the French surrender. He wrote of the Indians' reaction to the event:

They seemed amazed at the submissive salutations of the inhabitants, expressed their satisfaction at our generosity in not putting them to death, and said they would always for the future fight for a nation thus favored by Him that made the world.

Rogers recorded that milestone in the history of Michigan in his *Journals* of his experiences in the French and Indian War, published in London in 1765. That work was the first of three diverse volumes he would write during his brief but significant literary career.

Born at the frontier settlement of Methuen, Massachusetts, in 1731, Rogers grew into a tall and extremely powerful man while working the family farm and roving the wilderness as a hunter and trader. He saw his first military service at the age of 15, impressed into the militia to combat Indian raiding parties.

Following the death of his father, who was

mistaken for a bear and shot by a hunter in 1753, Rogers dabbled in crime by passing counterfeit colonial currency. When the scheme turned sour, to escape punishment he joined a New Hampshire regiment in 1755. That would not be the last time Rogers got into trouble with the law. Nevertheless his leadership, fighting and scouting abilities brought him a rapid rise in rank, to captain in 1756 and major two years later.

The daredevil raids he led into Canada and his powess in fighting Indian style made him the talk of colonial and London society. The techniques for wilderness warfare he drilled into his rangers remain models for partisan troops to this day. Following the Fall of Quebec, in recognition of his extraordinary service British Commander in Chief Jeffrey Amherst assigned Rogers the arduous task of accepting the surrenders of the French posts which lined the Great Lakes frontier. He accomplished his delicate mission ably with the exception of Fort Michilimackinac which he was unable to reach because of ice on Lake Huron.

Rogers returned to Detroit again in 1763, as part of a force sent to relieve the fort, then under siege by Pontiac's followers. During a foray against the Indians he narrowly missed the tragic fate that befell scores of other British soldiers during the engagement known as Bloody Run.

The following two years, saw Rogers sink into dissolution and debt. Unable to win advancement because of the resulting bad reputation he earned among his American superiors, he resigned his commission and sailed for London where he hoped to secure a better position through political channels.

The dashing ranger who sometimes sauntered down the streets dressed in his green leather uniform became the toast of London society. His hard drinking, hard fighting exploits won him new glory.

Detroit shown here in 1796 would have differed little from the city that Robert Rogers accepted from the French in 1760.

Once, while Rogers traveled across Hunslow Heath, a highwayman stopped the coach and, thrusting his pistol through the window, demanded the passengers to hand over their valuables. While the others reached for their purses, Rogers grabbed the startled robber by the collar, yanked him through the window, ordered the coachman to drive on and turned his captive in for a tidy reward.

In addition to campaigning for a lucrative political appointment, Rogers also sought to capitalize on his popularity and earn some much needed money via the pen. He polished up his journals covering the years 1755-60 and published them in October 1765 under the imprint of J. Millan, "Bookseller, near Whitehall."

Before the month was over, Millan, had also printed Rogers' second book, *A Concise Account of North America,* a compendium of the geography, history and natural history of the region from Nova Scotia to the Carolinas and from New York to Michigan. Based on his own observations while ranging those far flung frontiers, Rogers' book provided, in the words of a contemporary reviewer, "the most satisfactory description we have yet been favored with of the interior parts of the immense continent which victory has so lately added to the British empire."

Perhaps the most important contribution of Roger's *Concise Account* is his discussions of Indian culture. Despite having spent most of his life fighting the tribesmen, Rogers offers a sympathetic and often admiring view of their way of life. He thought their ethics, respect for the aged, parenting and control of passions, with the exception of revenge, "surpassing all but the most christian philosophers."

In contradiction to some later reports, such as that of Ohio surveyor Edward Tiffin, which disparaged Michigan, Rogers wrote:

The country between the lakes, and even much further north than Detroit is level, the soil excellent, the climate healthy and agreeable, and the winters moderate and short. Its natural productions are numerous and valuable. It is sufficiently, but not too thickly timbered; what there is, is tall and fair, and fit for any common use. In short, no country in any quarter, if any in the world, is capable of larger or richer improvements than this.

The critics lavished praise on Rogers' *Journals* and *Concise Account*. But upon venturing into a different genre, drama, his literary career came to a disastrous close. In February 1766, Millan published anonymously Rogers' *Ponteach: or the Savages of America. A Tragedy*. Tragedy is was, for the playwrite, that is. The press united in condemning it as "one of the most absurd productions we have ever seen."

Ponteach ranks as the second play to be written by a native New Englander and the first to use Michigan as a probable setting. And contemporary flop that it was, the play nonetheless offers for the historian valuable testimony based on Rogers' frontier observations including picturesque, descriptions of the methods used by unscrupulous traders to cheat the Indians:

But the great Engine I employ is Rum,
More powr'ful made by certain strength'ning Drugs,
This I distribute with a lib'ral hand,
Urge them to drink till they grow mad and valiant;
Which makes them think me generous and just,
And gives full Scope to practise all my Art.
I then begin my Trade with water'd Rum,
The cooling Draught well suits their scorching Throats.
Their Fur and Peltry come in quick Return:
My scales are honest, but so well contriv'd,

That one small Slip will turn Three Pounds to
One;
Which they, poor silly Souls! ignorant of
Weights
And Rules of Balancing, do not perceive.

Rogers' was spared at least an immediate sense
of his dramatic failure because when the play came
out he had returned to America. His political
connections had resulted in his appointment as
commandant of Fort Mackinaw, then located at
present day Mackinaw City.

Unfortunately, that position brought personal
tragedy for Rogers. His mismanagement of his
command, continued dissolution, fights with fellow
officers, disobedience to superiors and attempts to
feather his own nest via the Indian trade resulted in
his court martial for treason two years later. Acquitted
of that charge through lack of evidence, nevertheless,
Roger's life continued to slide downhill.

Back in England he spent a stint in debtor's
prison. Returning to America in 1775 and unable to
commit himself as a Loyalist or Revolutionary, he was
finally arrested by Gen. George Washington as a spy.
Rogers made his escape and raised a force of rangers
for the British. Defeated in a skirmish near White
Plains, he lost his command. His wife divorced him in
1778 and Rogers returned to England where he died
in poverty in 1795.

Eclipsing the wretched finale of the old
ranger's life are his prophetic statements in the book
he had written 30 years before about the land he
loved. He concluded his *Concise Account* with "In a
word, this country wants nothing but that culture and
improvement, which can only be the effect of time and
industry, to render it equal, if not superior, to any in
the world."

Hell on the High Seas:
The Saga of Joseph Bates

The old sea captain sleeps beneath the sod of Poplar Hill Cemetery, located north of Allegan on County Road A-37, halfway between South Monterey and Monterey Center. Don't blink while you're passing through either of those Allegan County communities or you'll miss them.

Shaded by ancient pines and maples and a copse of young walnut trees, a modern monument marks, anachronistically, the graves of Joseph Bates and his wife Prudence who died in the 1870s.

The back of its gray granite surface bears the chiseled rudiments of his life - that he was a sea captain, a pioneer health reformer and one of the founders of the Seventh Day Adventist Church. But those stony words do not hint at the maritime adventures that befell him during his 21 years on the high seas.

To hear the roar of a northwester, the flap of canvas as a puny sailing vessel runs before the storm's fury, to feel the swell of mountain high waves and the sting of salt spray you need to read the autobiography he penned between 1858-1863, a narrative befitting the plot of a Douglas Fairbanks movie.

Born in Rochester, Mass., on July 8, 1792, Bates moved with his family the following year to nearby New Bedford, famous in the annals of New England shipping. Like many another youth who grew up in that port, he yearned to become a sailor. At the age of 14, he signed on as a cabin boy, and sailed from New Bedford to London, England. His maiden voyage went smooth enough but on the return trip he fell while climbing the rigging at a height of 50 feet into the sea. He was rescued but that

34

mishap would prove but a pale shadow of what was to come on subsequent voyages.

His very next trip, in fact, brought him grief. While sailing from New York to Archangel, Russia, in mid May, his vessel encountered a field of icebergs. Just as the crew thought they had escaped the danger, a dense fog set in. Several hours later came a "dreadful cry from the helmsman - 'An island of ice!'" The ship crashed into an iceberg, wrecking everything on deck forward of her foremast. Miraculously, the vessel managed to break loose and limp to Ireland where repairs were made.

Resuming the voyage to Russia in company with a convoy of merchant ships protected by British warships, the fleet encountered a violent gale which blew many of the vessels ashore. Bates' craft narrowly escaped a similar fate by running before the wind. Just as the crew were congratulating themselves on their splendid seamanship, two Danish privateers captured the vessel. Towed to Copenhagen, the ship was forfeited to the captors in accordance with Napoleon's decree concerning any vessel doing business with the British.

A few weeks later Bates and the other crew members were called into court to give testimony concerning the voyage. A co-owner aboard had promised the men a handsome reward for lying that the ship had sailed directly from New York to Copenhagen.

Young Bates was the first to testify. The judge pointed toward a little box and said, "That box contains a machine to cut off the two fore-fingers and thumb of everyone who swears falsely here." "Now," said he, "hold up your two fore-fingers and thumb on your right hand and swear to tell the truth."

The little box worked wonders in eliciting truthful statements from Bates and the other crew members and they were exonerated. Later, while

The old Sailor, Joseph Bates, in 1868.

passing through the prison, they encountered the crew of a Dutch vessel, who evidently had not been so truthful. They thrust out their hands, lacking the thumb and two fore-fingers, through the cell bars in despair.

Bates eventually managed to make his way from Denmark to Ireland, although in the process he experienced a miserable voyage under "a cruel, drunken, parsimonious captain who denied us enough of the most common food allowed to sailors." From Belfast, Bates and two other crew members crossed to Liverpool to seek passage back to America.

Two days later, on April 27, 1810, as luck would have it, they were seized by a "press-gang" and shanghaied, or impressed, as it was called then, into the British Navy. Next came two years of Hell on the high seas as Bates repeatedly made escape attempts and conducted starvation strikes, making life miserable for himself as well his captors. Yet, despite all his appeals that he was American, it was "once in the navy always in the navy."

Impressment of American sailors, in fact, became one of the dominant causes, as articulated by President James Madison, for the declaration of war against Great Britain in 1812. Upon learning of that declaration, Bates and several thousand other Americans who had been impressed declared themselves prisoners of war rather than fight against their country.

At first herded onto prison ships under dreadful conditions, after several escape attempts the American seamen were ultimately consigned to an even more precarious existence in Dartmoor Prison. Following the Treaty of Peace in 1815, Bates and those others who managed to survive finally found freedom.

Bates returned to the sea, experiencing many more hair raising adventures during voyages to South America and exotic islands. He took time off from his world wanderings to marry the daughter of a Fairhaven, Mass., ship captain, Prudence Nye, in 1818. Bates ultimately rose to the rank of captain himself and commanded many a vessel before retiring from the sea forever in 1828.

Thirty years later, having taken up the cause of Adventism following the wreckage of the colorful Millerite movement that spawned it, he moved his family to Michigan. In 1860, he became the first pastor of the newly created Seventh Day Adventist Church in Monterey Township.

His faithful wife Prudence, who had spent many a night on a New Bedford widow's walk, died in 1870. Two years later the old sailor was laid next to her, far from the sea, in rural Monterey Township - with his thumb and two fore-fingers intact.

Leonard Slater, Indian Missionary

To the 300 Ottawa refugees who followed him to a new mission site in Prairieville Township, southern Barry County, he was spiritual guide, counselor and friend. Leonard Slater would spend over a quarter of a century endeavoring to protect his Indian flock from the "exploitations of the greedy, rum-selling white man." Though in the end he would be largely unsuccessful, he fought a noble battle.

At the age of 24 Slater launched his career as a Baptist missionary in 1826. Traveling via the Erie Canal, stagecoach and Lake Erie steamer, he and his wife made the arduous eleven days journey from Worcester, Mass. to Detroit. It took another nine days on horseback to reach their destination, the Carey Mission at Niles, founded four years before by the Rev. Isaac McCoy.

En route they camped overnight at the future site of Kalamazoo, near Gurdon Hubbard's old fur trading post then occupied by a French trader named Numanville and situated approximately at the intersection of Patterson Avenue and Riverview Drive. Delighted with the beauty of the Kalamazoo River Valley, Slater remarked that he would like to return there to live someday.

Reaching the Carey Mission on September 27, 1826, Slater and his wife spent the succeeding winter and spring assisting McCoy in his efforts to Christianize, educate and acculturate in the ways of the white man some 60 of the local Potawatomi and Miami children. The following year, the Slaters were assigned to work among the Ottawa at the Thomas Mission founded by McCoy in 1826 and situated on the west bank of the Grand River at present day downtown Grand Rapids.

Within a few years the tide of western immigration brought hordes of settlers and land speculators to the Grand River Valley. Grand Rapids, long the site of an Indian Village, developed into a thriving frontier town through the efforts of founding fathers Louis Campau and Lucius Lyon.

Slater played an active role in the growth of the pioneer community. In 1832, he became its first postmaster. A pigeon hole in his desk at the mission or his coat pocket sufficed for the entire community's mail. The mission school he operated served as Grand Rapids' only educational institution for nearly a decade. The white settlers ferried their children across the river to learn their "readin, writing and arithmetic" side by side with the Indian youths. Slater also campaigned to get the Baptist sponsored Michigan and Huron Institute located in Grand Rapids. Instead, that plum went to the little community on the Kalamazoo River then known as Bronson. Over the decades it would evolve into Kalamazoo College.

Meanwhile, increasing numbers of land lookers were casting covetous glances at the Ottawa land to the north of the Grand River. In 1836, the Ottawa finally signed away much of their homeland with the provision that they be allowed to remain on specified sites. But the burgeoning growth of Grand Rapids and the wiles of traders who fleeced the Indians of their treaty payments in exchange for firewater made the continuing existence of the Thomas Mission untenable

McCoy favored moving the Michigan Indians across the Mississippi, far from the evil influence of unscrupulous white men. Most Indians, quite understandably, preferred their native land to the windswept, treeless, prairies of Kansas, the domain of their ancestral enemies the Sioux.

Slater broke with McCoy on that issue and in late 1836 relocated his 300 followers on an 80 acre

The Rev. Leonard Slater, Indian Missionary to the Ottawa.

41

tract they had purchased between Indian Lake and Long Lake in southwestern Prairieville Township. A log cabin served as the first school and church at the "Slater Station." But by 1840 Slater had constructed a frame church that doubled as a school building complete with a steeple and bell.

Slater's work at the mission was not without its dangers. His daughter, Mrs. S.E. St. John, recalled in a Michigan Pioneer Society article that the Indians:

Sometimes, when drunk, they would come to kill father. One was sick and sent for father to come and cure him, but gave him to understand that if the medicine did not cure him he would kill him. Their idea seemed to be to get even with everyone, good for good, evil for evil: nothing was harder for them than to forgive their own injuries.

Prominent among Slater's converts was the distinguished Chief Noonday who had accompanied him from Grand Rapids. A "taciturn, dignified, commanding person" Noonday had fought bravely on the side of the British during the War of 1812. He had participated in the Battle of the Thames in 1813, witnessing the death of Tecumseh. Described in 1838 as "six feet high, broad shouldered, well proportioned, with broad, high cheek bones, piercing black eyes, and coarse black hair which hung down to his shoulders," even in his eighties Noonday possessed great strength.

Noonday's wife on the other hand offered a "Mutt and Jeff" foil for her aristocratic husband. Frank Little, a Richland pioneer, recalled her appearance:

Her ladyship, Mrs. Noonday, was a short, dumpy, unassuming lady of the old school. Nature had not see fit to make her very attractive by the bewitching fascinating charms of personal beauty but what little there might have been of feminine comeliness in her features had been sadly marred by an ugly scar on the left side of her face.

Slater, who had learned the Ottawa language, delivered his sermons to the Indians in their own dialect, invariably taking the precaution of practicing before Chief Noonday to get his criticism on pronunciation.

Slater's Barry County mission prospered for a decade or so, but following the death of Noonday in 1845 or 1846 and the inroads of land hungry settlers, his Indian flock gradually melted.

In 1852, Slater moved to Kalamazoo, returning on occasion to preach to the few Indians who remained at the mission. Soon they too scattered and all traces of the mission were obliterated. In Kalamazoo Slater also devoted his efforts to the Black citizens of that community.

He died in 1866, his last words being "Bury me by the Kalamazoo, on the spot where I first spread my tent and slept by the Indian trading post, on the night of my coming to the Mission." Accordingly, he was laid to rest in Riverside Cemetery, near the site of the old trading post. His friend, Chief Noonday, is commemorated by a road and a lake in the Barry County State Game Area.

The Bark Covered House

His calloused hands knew well the feel of the ax handle, flail and ox yoke. He could plow a furrow straight as an arrow and mow by hand a field of waving grain with the best of them. A man of tremendous strength William Nowlin had once pitted himself against a mechanical hayloader and with pitchfork and muscle beat the machine hands down.

Nevertheless, in 1875 Nowlin turned over to other men the management of his prosperous farm near Dearborn and spent most of the winter with his big right hand curled around a pen. Although he had received no formal education after the age of 12, the farmer had determined to set down his recollections in order to honor the achievements of his parents in carving a homestead out of the Michigan wilderness four decades before. The story he scratched out that winter captures a prime account of Michigan pioneer life - unexcelled in terms of authenticity, colorful descriptions and drama.

Privately printed for Nowlin in a small press run by the Herald Publishing House of Detroit in 1876 for distribution to friends and relatives, by the 1930s *The Bark Covered House* had become a rare and valuable volume, topping the desiderata list of many an advanced collector of Americana. J. Christian Bay, a famous Chicago bookman, wrote in 1935: "Each man has some luck, and deserves it, provided he is game when pure luck ceases. In all the many auction sales of Americana which we have had since the Great War, there has figured but one copy, which I luckily obtained, of a Michigan pioneer narrative entitled *The Bark Covered House...* To secure this was indeed luck. A splendid narrative, full of fine accounts of pioneer life and belief, hard struggles and quaint joys. There are one or two copies in Michigan, but I never traced a copy anywhere else." Fortunately for readers, R.R. Donnelley and Sons Co. republished the volume, edited and with an introduction by Milo Quaife, as its Lakeside Classic for 1937.

While the experiences related by Nowlin undoubtedly mirror those of many of the other pioneers who streamed into Michigan in the 1820s and 1830s, relatively few took the effort to record their day to day struggles amid the big trees and wild animals. Like so many of the Michigan pioneers, the Nowlin family saga began back in New York state. Barely able to scratch a living for his wife Melinda and their five children from a rocky farm in Putnam County, New York, John Nowlin realized his only hope of getting ahead lay on the frontier. William Nowlin remembered his father began to talk continually about Michigan Territory in 1831 or 1832. The family's reluctance to leave familiar surroundings for a strange new land where they would probably "be killed by the Indians, perish in the wilderness, or starve to death" could not influence the head of the house once he had made up his mind to go to "Michigania."

Nowlin sold his farm, bought a new rifle and shotgun, spent a couple of days practicing his aim, then left his family in a rented house while he set out "to view" Michigan in 1833. Six or eight weeks later he returned with news that "Michigan was a beautiful country, that the soil was as rich as a barnyard, as level as a house floor, and no stones in the way." He had bought 80 acres of government land at the going price of $1.25 an acre in Dearborn Township, twelve miles west of Detroit.

The Nowlins spent the winter of 1833 and 1834 with relatives to the west and in the spring of 1834 started in earnest for their new home in Michigan. They traveled via the Erie Canal, that great immigrant's highway which had since its completion in 1825 done so much to stimulate the ensuing Michigan land rush, to Buffalo. There they boarded the new steamer, *Michigan*. A furious storm nearly sent the Nowlins and the 600 other passengers on board to the bottom of Lake Erie before they stepped onto the wharf at Detroit, a bustling frontier "metropolis" containing 5,000 residents.

The family moved in with a neighboring settler while Nowlin began hewing logs for their cabin. A party of men from Dearborn, then known as Dearbornville, helped raise the logs. Nowlin roofed the little dwelling with black ash bark, hence the title of his son's book, and two weeks after they had arrived the family moved into their home, proud that they "had a farm of our own and owed no one."

Shortly thereafter, Nowlin bought an adjoining 80 acres in his wife's name. Both tracts were densely covered with hardwood giants: beech, hard maple, basswood, oak, hickory, tulip poplar, ash and elm. But to the pioneers that majestic forest was the enemy, a foe that needed to be beaten down for the sake of survival. The crosscut saw had yet to make its appearance in the Michigan woods so trees were felled solely through the swinging of the axe. Nowlin with his seven pound axe and 12-year-old William with a smaller weapon launched a relentless campaign against the trees, hacking away all day long at trunks 100 feet tall and as large as six feet in diameter. Weeks of toil won the pioneers a clearing of several acres that allowed them to see the sun from ten in the morning until one or two in the afternoon.

Nowlin purchased an ox team to help snake the logs off the clearing and then he planted corn, potatoes and a vegetable garden. The first year brought a meager harvest. The soil was very fertile, but too shaded. Season after season the war against the forest continued as the Nowlins claimed their homestead from nature through sweat and toil. The

46

waste seems staggering in present ways of thinking. Nowlin and thousands of other pioneers simply dragged and rolled the huge trunks into gigantic bonfires. By 1838 the family had cleared 60 acres and burned up "enough timber to have made five thousand cords of cordwood" (full cords 8 feet by 4 feet by 4 feet). That year the Michigan Central Railroad reached Dearborn and the wood burning locomotives finally produced a market for cordwood.

The nearly inpenetrable forest was not the only enemy the Nowlins faced. Clouds of mosquitos "vexatious, gory-minded, musical-winged, bold denizens of the shady forest," made life miserable for man and beast. The only way to keep the insects at bay lay in the continual burning of smudge fires in the clearing and within the log cabin at night.

Nowlin recalled other unwelcome guests who visited the interior of the cabin. A drunken bully of an Indian named John Williams once brandished his knife and announced: "I have taken off the scalps of six damned Yankees with this knife and me take off one more." The family lived in mortal fear for several years until the Indian died. The other dangerous visitor entered through a knot in the loosely laid flooring. While preparing dinner one evening every time Mrs. Nowlin stepped on a particular loose board she heard a strange rattling sound. She finally traced the sound to beneath a chest of drawers where lay coiled a big black rattlesnake prepared to strike. Fortunately the family killed the poisonous intruder before it could bite one of the children.

Nowlin recorded many other fascinating adventures in his book: encounters with bears and wolves, bee hunting exploits, the excitement over the Toledo War, William Henry Harrison's "log cabin and hard cider," presidential campaign of 1840, the arrival of the first Michigan Central locomotive and the horseman who raced the train and won.

47

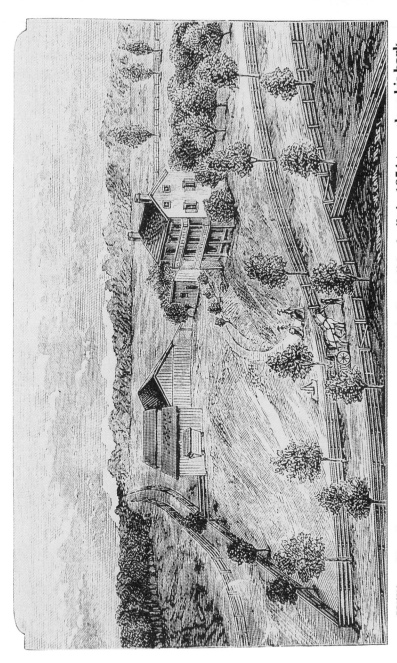

William Nowlin spent his last days at "Nowlin's Castle" he built in 1854 to replace his bark covered house.

With true pioneer fortitude the family, increased by the birth of another daughter, survived mosquitoes, drunken Indians, poisonous reptiles, dangerous animals and falling tree limbs known as widow makers, and in two years they moved into a larger house. Then the biggest threat to their continued prosperity emerged in the form of a mortgage. It was debt that nearly done them in. Against his wife's counsel Nowlin had borrowed $80.00 from a usurious widow to buy a pair of oxen. When the oxen died, Nowlin faced the nearly impossible task of making the yearly interest payment of $27.00 without the team to help him work. The family lived in fear of loosing their hard won homestead through foreclosure for several years. Finally William Nowlin was able to pay the debt off by hunting deer. The animals abounded and he became an expert hunter, killing as many as three or four a day and pulling sled loads to Detroit where the deer brought $2.50 to $5.00 apiece.

With the mortgage removed, which had been "like a cancer eating up our substance, gnawing day and night," the Nowlin's propects improved yearly. In 1854, the elder Nowlin built a substantial brick home known as Nowlin's Castle. There the old frontiersman "could sit on his veranda in the twilight, when it was pleasant... and peer away into the distance and see lights in different places glistening and shining like stars through the darkness. They were the lights of lamps and candles, burning in his distant neighbors dwellings." His son remembered that it had been three or four years after they had arrived in Michigan before the light of any neighbor's window could be seen from their house.

The old pioneer died in 1869 and Melinda was buried at his side four years later. Nearby in the Nowlin Cemetery sleeps the son who immortalized the family's pioneer experiences in a Michigan literary classic.

Klutzes on the Frontier

Picture the pioneer, sinewy and strong, rough hewn and tough as a panther, a rugged individual who with axe in hand boldly strode forth to subdue the wilderness. Guiding his covered wagon through the trackless forest, fighting Indians, wolves and bears, felling lofty trees, notching logs and single handedly raising his log cabin - it was all in a days work.

Undoubtedly there were many who actually fit that description - men among men. But what about the others, the not so tough and the not so strong, the timid, the clumsy, the backwoods bunglers. They too deserve a place in the history books and in the annals of the Kalamazoo River Valley's formative years several have indeed found their niche.

Three in particular come to mind, Oshea Wilder, Horace Wilson and one known simply "as a man named Sherwood." They all had one thing in common - they were frontier klutzes.

During the early 1830s an army of land hunters descended on Michigan like a plague of locusts. Some were genuine homesteaders seeking to carve a new life for themselves out of the wilderness. Many others, however, were simply speculators intent on buying up choice sections at the going price for government land, $1.25 an acre, and then selling out to later arrivals at a steep mark-up. The most ambitious of the speculators bought sites they thought destined to become towns, platted out streets and lots, and hoped to sell those lots for thousands of times what they had paid.

Soon, incipient cities dotted the length of the Kalamazoo River - Albion, Marshall, Battle Creek, Comstock, Kalamazoo, Pine Creek near Otsego, New Richmond and Singapore at the river's mouth. The founders of each thought their settlement destined to become the new metropolis of the northwest.

One of the most alluring sites on the Kalamazoo River comprised a peninsula formed by a series of horseshoe bends, as the river's big meanders were called. A fall of about eight feet in the river there promised excellent water power. What's more, it lay near the center of newly created Allegan County and therefore stood a good chance of being named county seat, an asset second deemed only to water power.

In the summer of 1833, two land speculators from Kalamazoo, Stephen Vickery and Anthony Cooley, bought from the government a portion of the land now comprising Allegan. Later that fall, George Ketchum, a speculator from Marshall, purchased another portion. In November, 1833, Elisha Ely, who hailed from Rochester, N.Y., toured Michigan looking for a good town site in which he and his son Alexander could invest. They bought from Vickery and Cooley a one third interest in their holdings. Together these various proprietors projected the village of Allegan.

Ely returned to Rochester where he recruited a contingent of friends and relatives, including Leander Prouty and his family, to pioneer in Allegan. They traveled via the Erie Canal and Lake Erie steamship to Detroit. There they purchased a yoke of oxen and wagon, piled it high with household goods, tools, equipment and supplies and made their way along the old Territorial Road to Bronson, as Kalamazoo was then known.

There being no road to Allegan, they loaded their goods and a supply of lumber to build shanties on two rafts, intending to float down the Kalamazoo River. Prouty, who had been a sailor in his youth, steered one of the rafts. The other - well that is where klutz number one, the man named Sherwood, enters the story. He took charge of the second raft. "Before the little squadron had proceeded far on its journey,"

The Michigan frontier beckoned to skilled men and klutzes too.

Prouty later recalled, Sherwood's craft capsized. Into the drink went their barrels of pork, flour, salt and other frontier necessities. They managed to retrieve some of the items, but one of the most essential, their only plow, remains somewhere on the muddy bottom of the river, probably to this day.

Eventually the Proutys arrived safely at their destination. They soon erected the first structure in Allegan. But Sherwood, having won his place in history through bungling, seems never to have never been heard from again.

Without his assistance, apparently, the tiny settlement prospered. The pioneers raised log cabins and dug a mill race. In 1835 the village was first surveyed and lots platted out. That is when klutz number two, Oshea Wilder, made his appearance. The initial survey job he performed turned out to be so woefully inaccurate that two years later another survey was required. Flavius Littlejohn provided a much more accurate survey but because he was forced to work in accordance with the erroneous lot lines already laid out, the village streets acquired a decided crooked nature.

Wilder, incidently, moved on from Allegan to found the ill-fated town of Singapore at the mouth of the Kalamazoo River. It was destined to be swallowed up by sand dunes, decades later.

Klutz number three, Horace Wilson, another native of Rochester, N.Y., arrived in Allegan in 1835. He immediately busied himself chopping down the giant trees that covered what is now the business district. Having accomplished that task he rolled the logs into an enormous pile and set it afire. Hardwood being virtually worthless that was a normal procedure for clearing land in pioneer days. Wilson, however, made a slight miscalculation as to the size and location of his bonfire. It blazed out of control, setting fire to several nearby residences as well as the community's newly constructed and only church, which burned to the ground. "Mr. Wilson," the compiler of the 1880 Allegan County History noted, "seems to have been satisfied with his latest achievement, for he soon after left the allurements of village life."

Somehow Allegan survived its klutzs. The Prouty family managed to borrow a plow from some friends in Otsego and got their first crop of potatoes in on time for harvest that year. Citizens rebuilt the church, as a matter of fact the community now worships at more than 20 of them. Wilder's crooked streets? They still serve as a memorial to the heroic pioneer days - when men were men - but not all of them good surveyors.

Pioneer Tourists Canoe to the Pictured Rocks

The great lake worshipped by the Chippewa as Gitchee Gumee had vented its rage in a gale the night before. Now it lay serene, as if exhausted from its efforts. Boldly, a birch bark bateau glided past the caverns and cliffs of the Pictured Rocks, east of present day Munising.

It was a September morning in 1835 and the canoeists, five French Canadian and Indian voyageurs and their passengers, a pair of refined New York gentlemen, gazed in absolute awe at the grandeur before them. Dr. Chandler Robbins Gilman, who shared with his traveling companion and brother the honor of becoming the first known tourists to visit Lake Superior, was moved to write:

> Nothing I had ever heard had at all prepared my mind for the sublimity and beauties of this scene; - the rock, so lofty and precipitous; the wide openings that yawned below, leading we knew not where; but above all the brilliant colours that diversify every foot of this vast range of rocks, now that we saw it lighted up by the sun's direct rays, it far surpassed brilliancy and beauty anything we had imagined...

Gilman penned that description in a two volume travel narrative published in 1836, *Life on the Lakes: Being Tales and Sketches collected During a Trip to the Pictured Rocks of Lake Superior.* Produced in a small edition and yet to be reprinted, the volumes have grown increasingly scarce (they now fetch $500 to $800 depending on condition). More is the pity, because Gilman's work contains some of the finest first hand observations of Michigan in 1835 by a gifted and insightful writer.

Born in Marietta, Ohio, on September 6, 1802,

Gilman sprang from stock who pioneered the Buckeye State. He attended college at Andover and Harvard and then earned his medical degree from the University of Pennsylvania in 1824. He soon located to New York City where he dabbled in journalism prior to carving out a notable career as a professor at the New York College of Physicians, a position he held up to his death in 1865. His numerous publications include treatises on gynecology and medical jurisprudence, long-forgotten tomes. His Michigan travel narrative, however, merits a better fate.

Gilman and his brother, referred to in the narrative only as "the Major," began their "tour of pleasure" on August 19, 1835. After steaming up the Hudson River, they slowly made their way across New York via horse-drawn canal boat along that immigrant's highway to "Michigania," the Erie Canal. Boarding the *Thomas Jefferson*, a "large and splendid boat," the travelers reached Detroit eight days after leaving New York.

Gilman found Detroit "very beautifully situated," but in "quite an uproar" over the prospects of a bloody campaign against Ohio to protect the "Toledo Strip." President Andrew Jackson would soon defuse that explosive situation and fortunately the Toledo War ended with but minor blood letting. Ohio got the strip and Michigan as a consolation received the western two thirds of the Upper Peninsula. While at Detroit Gilman, a temperance advocate, also sadly commented that the city's population contained "a much larger proportion of Irish than will ever be of benefit to the Territory," an allusion to the popular ethnic stereotype of the hard drinking "shanty Irish."

Sailing from Detroit on the schooner *White Pigeon*, Gilman did not reach Mackinac Island until five days later due to bad weather. He tarried several

Gilman's 1836 travel narrative included a print of the Pictured Rocks.

days on the "fairy island," delighted with its historic and picturesque aspects. He noted, however, that the local economy was a far cry from the glory days of the fur trade, due to the removal of the American Fur Company's headquarters to La Pointe, Wisconsin. Following a visit with resident Indian agent Henry Rowe Schoolcraft, who showed the visitors to the future "Wolverine State" one of the fierce animal's pelts, the tourists borrowed a canoe from the fur company and engaged five voyageurs to convey them to their destination, the Pictured Rocks.

After paddling through the Les Cheneaux Islands, the travelers camped for the night at De Tour, opposite Drummond Island. Buffeted by winds the next day, they were forced to put ashore on Lime Island to regum the seams of the bateau. Gilman penned detailed descriptions of what he saw, including the grave of an Indian chief on Lime Island. They made their way up the St. Marys River to Sault Ste. Marie, which Gilman thought "had a more flourishing look" than the village at Mackinac Island. To bypass the roaring rapids the voyageurs pulled their craft along the mile and a half long and 15 feet wide canal dug by the soldiers of Fort Brady. They pushed off for the most dangerous part of their journey - out into unpredictable Lake Superior.

Gilman provided a running narrative of the appearance of the coast line on the southern shore of Whitefish Bay: Iroquois Point, Rose Island, Naomikong Point and the mouth of the Waiska, Tahquamenon and Shelldrake rivers. He included several chapters describing his experiences at the settlement of Indian fishermen located at Whitefish Point. His book also contains a number of Chippewa legends set along Lake Superior which he heard first hand from the Indians and voyageurs.

Following the culmination of his pleasure trip, the viewing of the Pictured Rocks, which Gilman felt well worth the hardships of voyageur travel, he returned east via Chicago and St. Louis. In his book Gilman encouraged others to "make a trip to the great lakes" providing they were not "constitutionally timid." The Indian country," he warned, "is the worst place in the world for cowards, and if you are not absolutely frightened to death you will be alarmed at every step..."

As the succeeding decades brought easier access to the Lake Superior country, millions of tourists made similar pilgrimages to enjoy the Upper Peninsula's unspoiled beauty. And today it is still possible to embark on an armchair voyage back into Michigan's heritage via Gilman's delightful prose.

Yankee Lewis and His Famous Stagecoach Station

"If you are hungry and wish for a dinner,
Breakfast, supper and lodging to boot,
If you're a Turk, a Christian or sinner
Yankee Springs is the place that will suit..."

That's how George Torrey, assistant editor of the Kalamazoo *Telegraph* and self-styled poet, sang the praises of the famous hostelry operated by "Yankee" William Lewis at Yankee Springs, located two miles east of Gun Lake in western Barry County. Nor was he alone in regaling the Yankee Springs Tavern, an oasis of hospitality amid a wilderness of woods, wild animals and Indians.

In 1836, Lewis had loaded his family and possessions on a covered wagon to travel from western New York overland through Canada to a tract he had selected near South Bend, Ind. En route they stopped at a tavern at Gull Prairie, Kalamazoo County. There he learned from the landlord that a Calvin Lewis had settled as his closest neighbor in the woods 18 miles to the north. Lewis recognized his description as that of a long lost brother whom he thought dead.

The pleasures of his joyful reconciliation were exceeded only by his admiration of the splendid site for a tavern his brother had selected. Located on the ancient Indian trail that wound to Grand Rapids from one of the major east-west thoroughfares, the Territorial Road, now the approximate course of I-94, it seemed likely to develop into a important pioneer highway. Nearby a series of crystal clear springs bubbled up from the ground. The name Yankee Springs had been bestowed on the park-like site the year before by a group of travelers who chanced to camp there. That evening before the campfire they discovered they all hailed from New England.

Lewis promptly forgot about his South Bend destination, struck a bargain with his brother and soon he owned the 320 acre tract. The family moved into the primitive shanty that had been erected there and Lewis made a quick trip to Detroit for supplies for his new venture.

Soon, hordes of land-lookers from the east began pouring into the Grand River Valley and the Yankee Springs Tavern, then the only such facility within a radius of twenty miles in the wilderness did a "land office business." Lewis constructed a series of log cabin additions to the structure which he dubbed "the mansion house." Eventually it gained a reputation as the only seven story building in Michigan. All "seven stories" were on the ground. The building to the north was called the Grand Rapids room, while the most opulently furnished one to the south, the Kalamazoo room, often served as a bridal suite. In addition to the mansion house a half dozen or more other structures surrounded by a white picket fence comprised a virtual village.

To feed the many guests he entertained, sometimes as many as 100 a night, Lewis planted a four acre garden to the east of the tavern. He hired a young British immigrant skilled in vegetable growing, imported fancy seeds, constructed an irrigation system that ran from a hillside spring in hollowed logs and his garden became known as the best in the territory. Among the produce he grew were some of the first tomatoes and celery in Michigan. Reputedly Lewis even cultivated the peanut to perfection in "that quick, warm, rich, well-fertilzed sandy soil."

Lewis also hired the local Indians to supply him with venison, fish, cranberries and maple sugar, having wisely learned from a missionary to the Indians on the Grand River the words he would need to negotiate

An unknown artist painted the Yankee Springs tavern as it appeared in 1844.

with them. A smart businessman, he always bought what they brought whether he needed it or not, so as to encourage them to keep up the supply.

His wife Mary won fame as an excellent cook. One pioneer traveler remembered, "anyone who once partook of the savory viands served at his table would always make it a point to get to Yankee Lewis' tavern for entertainment." Eventually a stagecoach line was established and four stages a day stopped at the Yankee Springs "halfway house."

Lewis, a jolly, good natured man, was well remembered as an affable a host as ever greeted a load of bone-weary stage passengers. He seemed to never forget a face or a name, and guests always counted on a hearty handshake, a clap on the back and interesting conversation.

His guest register comprised a virtual roster of the leading figures in pioneer Michigan including governors Lewis Cass, Stephens T. Mason, Epaphroditus Ransom, Alpheus Felch and John Barry; the first state geologist Douglass Houghton, fur trader Rix Robinson, Grand Rapid's founder Louis Campau and circuit riding judge Flavius Littlejohn of Allegan.

Lewis was also known for his charity toward neighbors down on their luck. To tide them over he hired many of them to work his fields or build bridges and improve the road. It was, one early chronicler of Yankee Springs wrote, "no uncommon sight to see thirty or forty men hoeing corn for him and as many or more at work in his wheatfields on the same day."

By the 1850s, however, other highways, including the plank road which connected Kalamazoo and Grand Rapids via Plainwell, replaced the route through Yankee Springs as the major thoroughfare and business fell off.

Yankee Lewis died in 1853 at the age of 51 and, as had been his wish, the man "whose friends were many and his enemies few" was buried on a nearby hillside overlooking his beloved hostelry. His daughter later removed his remains to Grand Rapids.

Abandoned and allowed to deteriorate, all that remain of what was once the most famous hotel in southwestern Michigan are a few scattered foundation stones still to be seen about one quarter mile south of the intersection of County Roads 611 and 430.

Yankee Bill Lewis

Wolves Against the
Van Buren County Moon

Moon shadows etched a lacery of over-arching hardwood giants on the white mantled forest floor of the Van Buren County wilderness in 1836. Not a breath of air stirred the sharp still night.

It began with a low guttural groan, an eerie wail that grew higher and higher in pitch until it exploded in a burst of staccato yips. One by one answering howls harmonized into a blood-chilling chorus - the pack was astir.

That wild music had sent forest dwellers burrowing deeper into their nests since time immemorial. But now something was different. Scattered across the wilderness, a half a dozen or less to a township, lay tiny clearings crowned with log cabins. Pioneers from the east had arrived to battle the wilderness with axe, plow and rifle. And to those bold vanguards of civilization wolfen symphonies were definitely not music to the ears.

Wolf packs held sway over both peninsulas when the opening of the Erie Canal in 1825 and rumors of pristine prairies and parklike oak openings launched a land rush for "Michigania." Early settlers encountered two species of wild canines they termed wolves. The smaller brush wolves were actually coyotes. The much larger gray or timber wolves normally weighed between 70 and 100 pounds but prize specimens might double that size.

Wolves devoured seemingly anything and everything they encountered during their prowls including fish, fruit, insects, snails, birds and mammals of varying size. In winter wolves banded together into hunting units of three to a dozen or more. Emboldened by the strength of the pack and winter's hunger pangs they were capable of pulling down and devouring full grown deer, moose and oxen. And modern advocates of the theory that wolves will not attack man ought to read the Michigan pioneer record.

Jackson County pioneers, for example, found the scattered remains of an Indian hunter in 1836. Nearby lay the bodies of three wolves he had felled with his hatchet before the pack dragged him down. While such successful attacks on white settlers were rare, "Michiganders" recorded numerous examples of close calls.

The experiences of the hardy souls who pioneered Van Buren County, created in 1829 but without sufficient residents to establish an actual working government until 1837, offer a microcosm of what was happening statewide when white men first ventured into the wolves' domain.

Many a pioneer woman torn from eastern civilization to find herself struggling to keep family alive and her mind sane midst the Van Buren County forest primeval counted loss of creature comforts and social opportunities minor compared to the cold fear felt when the big wolves made their presence known. Henry Rhodes, for example, chopped out a little clearing in northwestern Paw Paw Township, raised a primitive log shanty and there in 1836 he brought his bride Laura. He left her there, alone, nearly a mile from the nearest neighbor, to manage the best she could while he plied his trade as a mason in the settlements. A half century later she still remembered with a shiver how the wolves' "nightly howls woke the echoes far and near."

Others recalled those wild serenades with a touch of humor. Young William Van Antwerp, the son of one of the earliest settlers in Antwerp Township, regularly practiced playing his flute each evening. David Schwartz, the first chronicler of Antwerp Township, wrote: "As soon as the melody commenced, the howls of wolves would resound from every side; when the flute stopped the howls would cease, but return with renewed vigor as soon as the music was recommenced."

The settlers of Porter Township thought the wolves "although numerous, were troublesome only as deprecators upon small live stock." Those in Lawrence Township remembered "the wolves used to howl about the cabins in an apparently very fierce manner, though really they were cowardly curs unless running in packs." Less reassuring as to that cowardly trait was the further recollection that "sheep, calves, and hogs were carried off sometimes in broad day by the marauding creatures, despite the utmost vigilance of settlers."

Lewis Johnson in adjacent Hamilton Township lost two calves to the wolves one dark night. Neighboring settlers set out with guns in response to the calves desperate bleatings, but to not avail. The annals of Hamilton Township abound with other "wolf stories." Zebina Stearns' two young daughters ventured into the woods to round up the cattle early one evening. They came upon the herd running terror stricken before a wolf pack. Their voices calmed the cattle down enough so that the equally frightened girls could each grab a bovine tail and be pulled home in safety.

Robert Nesbitt, who in 1835 became Hamilton Township's first settler, experienced an even closer call. While he walked home from Kalamazoo unarmed one bitterly cold night, a pack of ravenous wolves attacked. Nesbitt managed to scramble up a tree and from its top he could glimpse the light of his cabin about a mile away. As the wolves howled and snapped at the base of the tree, the half frozen pioneer determined to fight his way out of the predicament. He cut a stout bough, jumped to the ground and swinging right and left fought the pack off. He

Treed by the wolves.

sprinted toward home until the wolves gained on him and he went up another tree. Thus he desperately fought his way to his cabin which he reached "wellnigh worn out by the excitement and violent exertion."

William Murch, who arrived in Waverly Township in 1839, experienced a similar arboreal deliverance. While he walked to Breedsville during a driving snowstorm one evening, a wolf pack drove him up a tree. Afraid that he might fall asleep and fall "into the jaws of the hungry beasts," he tied himself firmly to the trunk with his handkerchief and there he spent the night, frost bitten but uneaten.

In addition to wandering around in the woods during snowstorms, some pioneers made other foolhardy mistakes that brought on wolf encounters. Fernando Annables settled in what was known as Clinch Township in 1836 and he later bestowed upon it the more euphonious name of Almeda. He set out from an Indian camp one night carrying on his shoulders two big venison hams he had traded. As might be expected, the wolves attacked. Annable ran for his life and though prepared to throw the hams to the pack he succeeded in reaching home in safety, hams and all. Decades later he recalled his adventure remarking "I was the worst scared young man you ever heard of."

Needless to say, the breed of man and women who left comfortable homes out east to brave life in the Michigan wilderness was not one to accept the threat of such wolf attacks passively. With the coming of the white settlers the days of the wolf in Van Buren County were numbered.

Among the earliest proceedings of the initial county and township governments were the creation of bounties on wolves and panthers. While a few panthers were seen, notably in Bangor Township, none appear to have been turned in for bounty. But with wolves it was a different matter. Coupled with a corresponding state bounty, wolf scalps could net a reward of as much as $30.00, although the exact amount varied geographically and with time. Thirty dollars during an era when a laborer might earn fifty cents for a ten hour work day and government land sold for $1.25 an acre offered a major inducement to hunt the wild canines.

Crisfield Johnson, the editor of the 1880 *History of Berrien and Van Buren County,* included a record of wolf bounties in that monumental publication so as to "portray the advance of civilization corresponding to the decrease in wolf slaughter."

In 1838 the Van Buren County Board of Supervisors awarded bounties for ten wolves killed. John Condon, a renowned hunter from Almeda Township who owned "a exceeding well trained wolf dog," turned in three scalps that season. Conspicuously absent from the list of bounty hunters that year, however, is the name of Daniel Pierce. A Kalamazoo resident who maintained a hunting cabin near South Haven, Pierce killed 13 wolves in 1838 and probably redeemed them in Kalamazoo County.

In 1839 the county and state bounties had been reduced by half, but still 24 wolves were credited.The years 1840 and 1841 each witnessed 13 wolf scalps redeemed and in 1842, 14 bounties were paid.

Hunters had by then made inroads on the wolf population and the number of bounties paid dropped dramatically - in 1843 to five, in 1844 none, 1845 nine, including five pups. Suspicions that some enterprising pioneers were raising wolf whelps for the bounty brought about a reduction in the value of pup scalps that year.

In 1846, the last year a Van Buren County bounty was offered, hunters took six wolves. The state bounty remained, however, and county pioneers continued to redeem a few wolf scalps each year. In 1852, an Indian named Joseph Mimtucnaqua slew the last known wolf in Van Buren County, Johnson thought it fitting that the deed had been performed "by one of the race of hunters who were long the lords of this land."

The last wild wolf in the Lower Peninsula was killed in 1909. In the Upper Peninsula the state bounty continued to claim victims until its repeal in 1960, with fewer than 20 wolves remaining. Now only on Isle Royale and in possibly a few other isolated sections of the Upper Peninsula does the wail of the wild continue to raise the hair on listeners' necks.

A Beautiful Red-Head
Visits the North Country

As if to honor the arrival of the lovely literary lady who had defied society's sanctions by journeying unchaperoned to the far reaches of the Great Lakes frontier in July, 1837, Mackinac Island had assumed one of her loveliest moods. Anna Jameson stood transfixed, enraptured by the beauty of the "fairy island." From the deck of the steamship *Thomas Jefferson* docked at the crescent shaped harbor she beheld:

On the east, the whole sky was flushed with a deep amber glow, flickered with softest shades of rose-color - the same intense splendor being reflected in the lake; and upon the extremity of the point, between the glory above and the glory below, stood the little Missionary Church, its light spire and belfry defined against the sky. On the opposite side of the heavens hung the moon, waxing paler and paler, and melting away, as it seemed, before the splendor of the rising day. Immediately in front rose the abrupt and picturesque heights of the island, robed in richest foliage, and crowned by the lines of the little fortress, snow white, and gleaming in the morning light. At the base of these cliffs, all along the shore, immediately on the edge of the lake, which, transparent and unruffled, reflected every form as in a mirror, an encampment of Indian wigwams extended far as my eye could reach either side.

Jostled from her revery by a fellow passenger, the Rev. Samuel A. McCoskry, Bishop of the Episcopal Diocese of Michigan, minutes before the steamer pulled away from the wharf, Jameson trundled her baggage down the gangplank with the bishop's help. More than a century and a half later the hordes of tourists that make a mecca of Mackinac encounter many of the same features described by Jameson during her sojourn there. That is, if you subtract the thousands of Indians who rendezvoused for their annual treaty payments and add the unique fragrance of horse droppings and fudge. One other major difference stands out. During her stay in 1837 Jameson shared Mackinac Island's many attractions with but one other resorter, an Irish woman from St. Joseph.

The tourism industry that would replace the fur trade as Mackinac Island's dominant economic activity had yet to make its appearance, chiefly because of lack of accommodations. Jameson found the only inn on the island completely full, but she was able to secure an excellent breakfast there of whitefish, eggs and tea, for which the metis woman proprietor charged her "twice what I should have given at the first hotel in the United States." Some things about Mackinac Island seem not to have changed.

Jameson had hoped to find lodging with resident Indian agent Henry Rowe Schoolcraft's family and later that morning when she called at the Indian agency building Schoolcraft warmly welcomed her to stay despite the sickness of his wife, Jane. Shortly before embarking from Toronto on her tour to the west, Jameson had been introduced to Jane's sister, Charlotte, wife of the Rev. William McMurray, Anglican missionary to the Indians at Sault Ste. Marie, Ontario. Jane and Charlotte were the daughters of Irish fur trader John Johnston and his Chippewa wife, Susan.

Despite having but a hurried visit prior to her steamship's departure Jameson had struck up a warm rapport with Mrs. McMurray, who promised her she would be welcome at her sister's home on Mackinac Island. That invitation and the prospect of perhaps visiting the McMurrays at Sault Ste. Marie had determined Jameson's itinerary to the Upper Peninsula. She might well have decided to travel overland to the west from Detroit as another British literary lady, Harriet Martineau, had the previous summer. But Jameson's fortunate choice in taking a northern tour resulted in her vibrant pen pictures of Michigan scenery, voyageurs, canoe travel and Indian culture, some of the most valuable and colorful description of that era.

Although not mentioned in the book she wrote about her travels, Jameson had another reason for leaving Toronto society for the rigors of the western frontier - her unhappy marriage to a cold hearted Toronto judge.

Born in Dublin, Ireland, in 1794, the eldest of five sisters, Anna Brownell Murphy, grew into a beautiful red-haired young lady, gifted, impetuous, and headstrong . As a teenager she led her sisters to defy the authority of their governess.

She was 26 when she met a young lawyer named Robert Jameson. A few months later they were engaged, but he soon broke it off. She nursed her wounded pride by making a grand tour of Europe as the governess of a wealthy family. In 1825 came a sudden reconciliation and she married Jameson. But most of the ensuing long unhappy relationship would be spent in separation.

Jameson began her literary career the following year with a journal of her European travels. She followed that success with more than 15 books about travel, art, and women. She also became friends with some of the leading writers and artists of the time.

When her husband was appointed to a high ranking judgeship in Canada in 1833, he left for Toronto without her. Against her better judgement, she joined him there in December, 1836. To escape his callous treatment of her and what she perceived as a

This 1870s view from Fort Mackinac had changed little since Jameson's visit in the 1830s.

pretentious Toronto society, she left for her western tour in June, 1837. Traveling overland to the village of Chatham on the Thames River, she boarded a steamer which carried her down the river and Lake St. Clair to Detroit.

A severe attack of illness, "the combined effect of heat, fatigue and some deleterious properties in the water at Detroit, against which travellers should be warned," marred her visit to the "City of the Straits." While incapacitated she missed her scheduled steamer and had to tarry an additional six days before the departure of the *Thomas Jefferson*. A pleasant two days voyage brought her to Mackinac Island.

Jameson found the many Indians encamped on the island of especial interest. She spent much of her time there walking among their encampments, poking her head into wigwams, shaking countless hands and replying "Bojou! Bojou!" and asking questions of the woman in particular. She liked the Indians and they liked her. They named her *Ogima-quay*, "the fair English chieftainess," in reference to her alabaster white complexion and auburn hair.

One afternoon some Indian braves staged a dance in her honor. Unlike her experiences in the beach camps, she found it a "grotesque and horrible phantasmagoria." She actually felt frightened when "these wild and more than half-naked figures came up, leaping, whooping, drumming, shrieking, hideously painted, and flourishing clubs, tomahawks, javelins, it was like a masque of fiends breaking into paradise."

Jameson also witnessed several examples of the baneful effects of firewater on the Indian temperament. And Schoolcraft told her an amusing anecdote relating to that topic:

A distinguished Potawatomi warrior presented himself to the Indian agent at Chicago, and observing that he was a very *good* man, very *good* indeed - and a good friend to the Long-

76

knives, requested a dram of whiskey. The agent replied, that he never gave whiskey to good men, - good men never asked for whiskey; and never drank it. It was only *bad* Indians who asked for whiskey or liked to drink it. "Then," replied the Indian quickly in his broken English, "me damn rascal!"

A highlight of Jameson's northern travels came when she seized the opportunity to accompany Jane Schoolcraft on a visit to her family in Sault Ste. Marie. They made the two day's journey in a bateau rowed by five voyageurs. Always eager for novel experiences, Jameson became the first European female to shoot the roaring rapids at the Sault in a birch bark canoe. The local Chippewa bestowed on her another name in honor of her feat - "Woman of the bright foam."

From the Sault, Jameson made her way back to Toronto, via Manitoulin Island, in a voyageur craft. Two months had elapsed since her departure. She returned to England and never reconciled with her husband. Upon her return she recorded her adventures in *Winter Studies and Summer Rambles in Canada* (3 vols., London, 1838). An American edition in two volumes was published in 1839 and an abridgement of her travel narrative appeared in 1852.

Jameson's lawyer husband died in 1854, leaving no provision for her whatsoever in his will. Head unbowed, she continued to write and immersed herself in charity work until her death six years later.

Michiganders can be grateful she left as part of her literary legacy such colorful descriptions of the pristine northland.

Dr. William UpJohn: Hastings' Beloved Pioneer Physician

They remembered Dr. William UpJohn as an expert horseman, a pioneer doctor who ate, slept and all but lived in the saddle while making his rounds through the Barry County wilderness. They remembered him riding off as surgeon of the Seventh Michigan Cavalry, Gen. George Armstrong Custer's regiment, in 1862. Nearly four-years-later he rode back into Hastings on the same faithful horse, having served in numerous Civil War campaigns and journeyed out west to fight Indians.

They remembered him as a generous man who saved many a pioneer's life through his medical acumen and never charged a penny if times were tough. They remembered him as his nephew W.E. Upjohn's mentor - back in the days before that young doctor invented a new fangled type pill that could be crushed under your thumb, thereby launching a pharmaceutical empire.

Perhaps most significantly, those who knew him remembered a man "possessed of most of the virtues and having but few of the faults of humankind, who has endeared himself to the people in such a way that his name has become a household word."

Born in Shaftesbury, England in 1807, the son of a wealthy civil engineer, Upjohn was the oldest boy in a family of 12 children. At the age of 21 he immigrated to America with brother Uriah. Five years later, the rest of the family followed, eventually settling in Monroe County, N.Y.

In 1831 William and Uriah began to study medicine under the tutleage of a local physician. Following two years attendance at the College of Physicians and Surgeons in New York City they received their medical diplomas.

Dr. William Upjohn, Barry County's beloved horseback doctor.

The chance for a new life in "Michigania" beckoned to the Upjohn brothers. as it did to many a fellow New Yorker, Arriving at the frontier settlement of Bronson, as Kalamazoo was then known, in 1835, they soon selected tracts of wilderness land near Richland, paying the going price to the government - $1.25 an acre. There Uriah launched the medical career which would span many decades and make him a beloved figured in Kalamazoo County annals. William, however, forsook the scalpel for the spade.

The practice in that region during those sickly times when most pioneers suffered the fever and shakes of the ague (malaria) proved too much for one man. So in 1837 William dusted off his black bag and joined his brother in the medical profession.

Four years later, William followed the blazed trail to Hastings where he treated a Mr. Leach, after whom nearby Leach Lake was named. On his return trip he stopped to minister to other sickly pioneers in Hastings,then but a little hamlet of 12 to 15 families established five years before. Upjohn decided to cast his lot with that promising community

He first hung out his shingle at Levi Chase's tavern located on the bank of the Thornapple River. Soon he moved into a dwelling on the southwest corner of Creek and Apple Streets. Later he built a house on State Street. His final home was at 120 S. Broadway. That structure was moved in the 1980s to the Charleton Park Historic Village and renovated.

During the first four years of his practice in Hastings, Upjohn was the only physician in the entire county. He spent many long nights riding to isolated log cabins, delivering babies, setting broken limbs, and doling out powders, pills and poultices.

In 1842, Upjohn married Affa Connett. Sadly, she died within the year. He had made a deathbed promise to her to take care of her younger sister Lydia Amelia. Taking that pledge seriously, he married his sister-in-law in 1847, and she bore him three daughters.

In addition to his far ranging medical practice, Upjohn played an active role in community affairs. In 1852 he was elected Barry County Register of Deeds and appointed to the Board of Regents of the University of Michigan.

Following the outbreak of the Civil War, Gov. Austin Blair commissioned Upjohn as surgeon of the Seventh Michigan Cavalry on November 1, 1862. He served with distinction in that famous unit, participating in Gen. Hugh Kilpatrick's ill-fated foray against Richmond and with Gen. William T. Sherman in the Atlanta Campaign. He won promotion to surgeon in chief of the First Brigade, First Division of Cavalry, Army of the Potomac.

When the war ended on May 26, 1865, the Seventh Michigan Cavalry became one of the unfortunate units ordered west to fight Indians. Upjohn rode with the regiment to Fort Leavenworth, Kansas, and from there across the plains to the Rocky Mountains. Not until November 7, 1865, was he discharged.

Returning to Hastings, Upjohn resumed his medical practice. Following graduation from the University of Michigan Medical School in 1875, William E. Upjohn, one of Uriah's 12 children, went to work for his uncle in Hastings. Several years later, he set up his own practice and in 1884 perfected his invention known as friable pills. Moving to Kalamazoo, W.E. Upjohn launched in 1886 the pharmaceutical firm that would ultimately make the family name world famous.

William remained in Hastings, dying there in 1887. "Beloved, honored and mourned by all" his fellow citizens.

Lewis Cass Crosses the Sea

No name commands more respect in the annals of 19th century Michigan than that of Lewis Cass. He fought valiantly in the War of 1812 - and rather than hand his sword over to the British following General Hull's controversial surrender of Detroit he broke it over his knee. He explored the uncharted reaches of the Lake Superior frontier, negotiated numerous Indian treaties and once strode unarmed into a hostile Chippewa camp at Sault Ste. Marie to yank down a British flag and trample it underfoot. For 18 years he guided Michigan through its territorial period before leaving for posts in Washington as secretary of war, senator and secretary of state. He served his country as minister to France from 1836-1842. He figured prominently in three presidential campaigns.

Yet all his patriotism and bravery could do little to protect his name before the power of the pun when a wag smirked that "it was impossible for Cass to cross the sea (C) without making an ass of himself."

New York lawyer and European gadabout Maunsel B. Field recorded the barb that sullyied the name of the great Cass in his *Memories of Many Men and of Some Women*, published in 1874. According to Field, the joke had been uttered in reference to "a rather weak book" written by Cass, about his impressions while he served as French ambassador *France, Its King, Court and Government* (New York, 1840). Setting aside his numerous printed speeches and pamphlets, that 191 page volume comprises Cass' only published book. Although it went through three editions by 1848, most contemporary reviewers seem to have agreed with Field, and the punster, that the work contained little of value.

Nevertheless Cass' sole book contains a great deal of significance for Michigan readers, not so much

GENERAL CASS.

This likeness of Cass that accompanied his 1848 presidential campaign biography almost assured he would not get elected.

for its analysis of French society as for what its pages reveal about the author's character, experiences and prejudices.

Cass' ministerial duties in Paris were not particularly demanding and he devoted his excess time and energy to the study of history, a subject that had long intrigued him. He hired a young college graduate to assist him in copying archival manuscripts pertaining to the French regime in North America and thereby launched the career of Pierre Margry, who became one of the foremost French historians specializing in that field. While Cass made little use of those records himself, he loaned then to Electa Sheldon of Detroit and they formed the basis of her *Early History of Michigan* (1856).

As his book reveals, Cass also valued oral history as a source. He spent many hours interviewing old veterans about their recollections of Napoleon and once chatted with a 90-year-old physician who had known Benjamin Franklin in Paris. Cass often tramped the winding streets and dirty alleys of Paris observing and conversing with the working class. One such slumming foray, afforded him an opportunity to demonstrate his frontier-bred coolness and courage. He had joined a crowd to observe a party of revolutionaries construct a street barricade when a troop of soldiers arrived. The demonstrators had already fled the scene, but the soldiers shouldered their muskets to fire a volley at the innocent spectators. Cass calmly strode up to the officer in charge, apprised him of the real nature of the crowd and thus averted a massacre.

While Cass found much in Europe of interest, in general, European institutions, society, table manners and even the scenery suffered in comparison to that of his native land. The Michigan frontiersman who had sampled the flamboyant fare of French royalty wrote: "I have ate many a meal in the woods without a fork, and never a more pleasant one than when cutting a piece of venison rib from the stake upon which I had watched it and roasted it before the fire."

Indeed, while touring the fabled Aegean Islands in 1837, he confided to his journal that his thoughts returned to "the entrance into Lake Superior, with the shores embossed in woods, the highlands gradually opening and receding on each side, and the water as clear as crystal, extending beyond the reach of eye, forms one of the most striking displays of natural beauties it has ever fallen our lot to witness."

In his book on France, Cass found the prospects for advancement of the European working class dismal as compared to those of America, where "every honest industrious man can... by emigrating westward procure a piece of land, and close his days surrounded by his family." His countrymen owed that fortunate state of affairs, Cass felt, to their political institutions, society and "to the advantages resulting from the situation of our country, connected with its capacity for the almost indefinite extension and comfortable support of the population..."

Cass, in fact, had played a significant role in accomplishing that potential for "manifest destiny," via his many treaty negotiations that for paltry payments extinguished Indian rights to their domain. In his book on France Cass penned, perhaps, a subconscious justification for the great aboriginal "land grab." In reference to an Indian chief's foiled attempt at stealing King Louis Philippe's favorite dog when he toured the New York frontier in 1797, Cass wrote: "one thing is certain, that from Hudson's Bay to the Gulf of Mexico very few Indians can be found who will not steal from a white man, when they are not apprehensive of detection, and who are not proud of cheating the Tshin-o-ke-mann (white man)."

Six Months Among the Indians In the Allegan Forest

Old Chief Sagemaw had imbibed a bit too much firewater. Darius B. Cook and his companion, James Rhodes, had plied the nearly 80-year-old Indian with liquor in order to loosen his tongue and hear a good story about the War of 1812. The white men got more than they had bargained for that winter's day in 1840.

Born in 1815, Cook had printer's ink in his veins. While a youth he worked as a printer's devil in Litchfield, Conn., and later honed his typesetting skills at the New York *Herald*, the *Saturday Evening Post*, Baltimore *Sun* and the Richmond *Enquirer*. In 1836 cook caught the Michigan fever and journeyed to the territory that was then experiencing a land rush of epic proportions.

The following year he secured a job with the Kalamazoo *Gazette*. Editor Henry Gilbert, who had moved the newspaper from White Pigeon to what was then called Bronson in 1835, evidently proved a hard taskmaster. Long hours of hand setting minute type by the light of flickering candles to make the weekly deadline and printing each sheet on a primitive Washington hand press wore the young man out. The 24-year-old printer had become so exhausted by November 1839 that he had resigned his position on the newspaper.

Fortunately he came under the care of Dr. Horace Starkweather. Other physicians of the time might have doled out to the pale and coughing young man harmful doses of strong drugs or have bled or leeched him but Starkweather offered some sage advice:

You want fresh air and exercise. Go live with the Indians, sleep in their wigwams on a bed of leaves, hunt in the forests, live as they live, and the chances are you will recover. Pure air, rarified by the trees in the forest, will do any man good.

Cook took the doctor's advice. Convincing his friend Rhodes to join him, the two secured a set of wolf traps, rifles and ammunition, provisions and equipment for camping, loaded all that, as well as half of a dead horse for wolf bait, on a bob sled drawn by a yoke of oxen and embarked on a winter's campaign among the wolves and Indians of the Allegan Forest.

Making their way across Gull Prairie to Yankee Springs, having passed but six cabins en route, the wolf hunters spent a night at Yankee Lewis' famous tavern. The following day they reached their destination, an abandoned log shanty near the present site of downtown Wayland.

Their first efforts at trapping wolves, on which the state and various townships and counties had levied lucrative bounties, proved disappointing. They secured nothing but the toes and feet of wolves, the desperate animals having bitten them off, Eventually they learned to set their traps tied to a grape vine which yanked the animals into the air, powerless to bite themselves.

In December, a band of Potawatomi encamped about a mile away. Among them was Adaniram Judson, who had been an interpreter for Gov. Lewis Cass at one time. Judson, "a fine specimen of the tribe" reputedly able to run down deer and cut their throat with his knife, befriended the wolf hunters. One morning, Judson led them to the wigwam of Sagemaw, located about three miles away, to cajole the old chief into telling about his exploits during the massacre and burning of Buffalo on December 29 and 30, 1813.

Sagemaw, who despite his age stood six feet tall and as straight as an arrow and "walked with youthful elasticity" remained taciturn until the white visitors produced a flask of whiskey. After the chief had gulped down several drams out of a bear's skull, he began to sing and dance.

His lips thusly loosened, Sagemaw began recounting his exploits during the War of 1812. Like most Michigan Indians he had taken the side of the British. He had fought at the Battle of the Thames on October 5, 1813, during which Gen. William Henry Harrison's troops revenged the River Raisin massacre at the site of Monroe earlier in the year. Sagemaw had seen the great leader Tecumseh killed and had helped carry his body from the battlefield. He showed Tecumseh's pipe to Cook and they later smoked from it.

A few more swallows of whiskey later, Sagemaw was ready to tell of the massacre at Buffalo. Following the British victory there, the Indians had rounded up "over 100 women and children." Separating the women, who were to be led away as captives, from the children, the Indians began tossing them into the burning buildings. Eyes glittering, Sagemaw told how he had taken the feet and another chief, Sunagum, the hands and swung young children into the flames where they writhed and screamed in agony.

About that time, the old chief leaped to his feet, gave a horrible war whoop and began brandishing his scalping knife and tomahawk in such a threatening manner that Cook and Rhodes backed out of the wigwam and cocked their rifles.

Fortunately Sagemaw's three squaws managed to calm the old man down and he dropped back onto his bear skin robe. Sagemaw then continued his story. The British cavalry had intervened and put an end to the murder of children. But Sagemaw managed to smuggle away a woman named Alice and a beautiful 12 year old girl named Effie.

Alice, who evidently was not as comely, met a

Cook's book about the Allegan Forest included a pictorial representation of the tragic fate of Alice, the Indian captive.

tragic end. The young bucks of the tribe tied her to a tree and used her for target practice. Shooting blunt arrows at an arm, a finger, an ear, a breast and other parts of her anatomy she was "bruised in a most shocking manner." Finally her eyes were shot out and prickly with arrows she was left "to be devoured by wolves."

Pretty Effie enjoyed only somewhat of a more fortunate fate. Adopted into the tribe, she was married to one of Sagemaw's sons and bore him five children before dying during child birth.

Following a feast of muskrat stew ladled into bear skull bowls, the wolf hunter's bid adeau to the old chief. Cook and Rhodes experienced many other adventures during their six months' stay in the Allegan Forest. They killed scores of wolves, deer, panthers, wildcats etc. and once rescued one of the old chief's wives from a wolf pack. Some of the exploits Cook recounted in the book he published in 1889 would, in fact, be well neigh unbelievable had they not come from the pen of a venerated newspaper editor.

Following his stint in the woods, which cured him completely, Cook worked for several other Michigan newspapers before settling down in Niles in 1842 as editor of the Niles *Republican* and later the Niles *Weekly Mirror* and Niles *Globe*. By the time of his death in 1901, he had gained the reputation as being "the oldest living member of the newspaper profession who had followed the business continuously in the state."

Olivet College & Other Episodes of A Life Well Spent

The Honorable Wilson C. Edsell sat at the massive rolltop desk, thoughtfully stroking his long white beard, as he gazed out the window of his second-story office one morning in 1880. Before him stretched a bustling downtown Otsego street scene. Carriages and farmers' wagons from the Allegan County hinterlands rumbled along, leaving wheel tracks in the dusty street. Housewives in search of bargains scurried by, deftly holding their long skirts just above the wooden sidewalks.

Edsell was oblivious to the commotion. His mind was 500 miles away and 50 years in the past. Once again, he was a bare-foot plowboy on his father's farm near Pike, Pennsylvania.

Seated in a chair near the desk, a young writer who had come to interview Edsell for a biographical piece to be published in *The History of Allegan and Barry Counties* nervously drummed his pencil against a notebook. "Mr. Edsell," he interjected, "I asked you of which of your accomplishments are you most proud?"

"I know you did, son. But that's a mighty tough question. Give me a few moments to cogitate," Edsell said slowly, as he returned to his revery.

Let me see, he thought, as he ticked off his accomplishments on his fingers. In 1869, I founded the first bank in Otsego with my son-in-law, H.N. Peck. I was a successful lawyer and a justice of the peace for 16 years. Twice I won election as state senator. I served on the Board of Trustees of the Kalamazoo Insane Asylum. I made a bushel of money through my Allegan County real estate investments as well as my insurance business. No, none of those things.

A few seconds later, he turned to the young writer, whose eyes had begun to glass over, and said. "Among the most prominent things of my life work and the most personally satisfying was the pleasure of taking care of my mother in her old age."

"She lived to be 94-years-old," he added proudly. "And then there were my untiring efforts in support of the anti-slavery movement and the organization and perpetuation of the Republican party in 1854. But there was one other thing of which I'm most proud. That was the part I took in the founding of Olivet College."

"Olivet College, between Marshall and Charlotte?" asked the writer, shaking away his lethargy.

"That's the one. Let me tell you about it. Now in 1835, I was 21-years-old. My total worldly assets numbered a strong pair of hands, a good constitution, three years' experience as an apprentice carpenter and five dollars in cash. I headed west, spending time in Cleveland, Sandusky and Monroe, Ohio, where along the way I became adept at building flour and saw mills."

"In Monroe I fell in love with Julia Cleck and we married in 1839. The following year we decided to pursue a college education together. About the only place in the country then that accepted women was Oberlin College, southwest of Cleveland So we enrolled there in 1840. By the way, where'd you go to school young man?"

The writer, who had started to slump forward in the chair, quickly jerked up, answering, "University of Michigan," sir."

"Aha! Well, back then, Oberlin had quite a reputation as the liberal center of the west. Why it even allowed blacks to attend. Some claimed it was

92

Wilson C. Edsell paid to have this likeness in the 1880 Allegan County History.

the hotbed of the anti-slavery movement."

"We got to know the college founder, Rev. John J. Shipherd, fairly well during our four years of study. I guess we picked up some of his radical ideas, too. Crazy notions, most folks thought, like sexual and racial equality."

"Well anyway, in 1843, Shipherd decided it was about time for him to establish another college like Oberlin. He made an exploratory trip up to Michigan. Riding through the wilderness in southern Eaton County one day, he got lost three times. Each time he wound up back on the top of the same beautiful wooded hill. He decided the Lord was telling him something. That was the spot for his new college."

"Shipherd returned to Oberlin and recruited colonists to launch his college in the forest. My wife and I decided we wanted to be a part of that adventure. So we and 37 other colonists made the trek to Michigan the following February"

"It was rough going those first few years, let me tell you that. We chopped trees from dawn to dusk, built log cabins, a church and a classroom and planted crops. Just as we were finishing the classroom, it caught fire and burned to the ground. That didn't stop us though. We built another one a couple months later."

"I supervised construction of a water powered grist mill and a sawmill that summer. We thought we were really in business. Then disaster struck. It was the rainiest season I've ever seen. The creeks overflowed and flooded the low land. Worse yet, that stagnant water bred mosquitoes by the millions. There was hardly a man, woman or child among us that didn't come down with the fever and chills of malaria - ague we called it then. That disease claimed the life of Shipherd, our guiding light, that first summer."

"We nearly all pulled up stakes and gave up.

About half the colonists left that first year, but my wife and I and some other stubborn souls stayed on. Olivet College opened in 1844 and despite every adversity imaginable we stuck to our guns. Why, the State Legislature even refused to grant us a charter, thanks in part to good old Senator Flavius Littlejohn from Allegan who was afraid we were going to promote abolitionism. But, by the time I left in 1849 to seek my fortune in Otsego the college was going strong and you can bet it still is."

"Yes sir, my boy, there's been a lot of water under the dam since then, but I've never done anything better than help get that college going."

Edsell glanced at the writer to get his reaction. Chin against his chest, he was fast asleep. Edsell nodded his head knowingly, "University of Michigan, indeed," he chuckled and turned back to his window to resume his revery of a life well spent.

Rev. John Pitezel's Upper Peninsula Missionary Life

The Reverend John H. Pitezel hobbled along through the Upper Peninsula wilderness of white. Each tortured step brought a grunt of pain. On a hurried 120 mile cross country trek from his Kewawenon Mission, near the present site of L'Anse, to Grand Island in January 1844, he had developed in his left ankle a case of *mal du raquette*, or snowshoe-lameness, caused from overstraining the tendons. Now during his return trip the Methodist missionary found walking so painful that he tied a thong to the front of his snowshoe which at each step he lifted with his left hand. "A hard way to walk," he admitted, "but it must be that or nothing." The following day, as he struggled on through the deep snow, the pain became so intense that he was forced to stop and make camp after only five miles.

Pitezel recorded his snowshoe ordeal and the many other adventures he experienced during his nine year stint as a missionary in the Lake Superior country in *Lights & Shades of Missionary Life...* published in 1857. Fortunately containing less than the usual amount of religious verbiage, the bane of missionary accounts, the pages of Pitezel's narrative offer rare glimpses of Upper Peninsula life during the watershed period of the 1840s.

During his quest for converts Pitezel ranged along much of the southern Lake Superior coast from Sault Ste. Marie to La Pointe, with forays as far as Sandy Lake, Minnesota. He recorded many examples of the Chippewa culture of the time and he witnessed the coming of the hordes of propectors in search of copper and iron that would ultimately transform the economy and character of the Lake Superior region. Pitezel's book also offers choice accounts of many of the colorful characters who made Upper Peninsula history: Douglass Houghton who inspired the Copper Rush of the 1840s; Philetus Church who founded a raspberry jam empire on aptly named Sugar Island; legendary fur trader Ramsey Crooks; Stephen Bungo, an Indian interpreter and one of the first blacks to figure in Lake Superior traditions; Henry Rowe Schoolcraft's wayward brother James and his probable murderer, John Tanner, the wild man of the Sault. And of course Pitezel provided numerous references to fellow clergyman, the Methodist preachers, Peter Doughtery, D.D. Brockway, W.H. Brockway; Baptist clergyman Abel Bingham, and others

The name of yet another missionary who angled for Indian souls in those same waters is conspicuously absent from Pitezel's narrative. Considered by the itinerant Methodist as a competitor rather than a colleague, Father Frederick Baraga is termed only "the priest." Baraga an Austrian who would win fame as "the apostle of the Chippewa," maintained his mission headquarters near L'Anse at the same time Pitezel was there. Rumors that "the priest" intended to conduct a proselytzing visit to Chief Monomonee's band on Grand Island had inspired Pitezel to rush there in January 1844 to ensure the Indians remained securely in his own fold. In company with two Indian guides Pitezel raced through the dense forest, crossed chains of little lakes, clambered along the rocky shores of Lake Superior and forced his through cedar swamps, while climbing over or creeping under masses of fallen brush and timber.

On the evening of the fourth day of travel the three reached the mouth of the Carp River, now the site of Marquette, the largest city in the Upper

Peninsula. There Pitezel found one solitary wigwam, the home of Marji-Gesick and his family. Pitezel and his campanions spent the night with the Chippewa family before treking the remaining 40 miles to Grand Island the following day. Marji-Gesick's wife served the weary travelers a venison dinner and graciously mended the missionary's mocassins that had worn completely through. Marji-Gesick would earn his niche in history 18 months later when he led Philo Everett to a mountain of iron ore near present day Negaunee. There Everett founded the Jackson Mine, the pioneer iron operation of the Marquette Range.

Pitezel found the Grand Island Indians "in a low state of religion." He spent several days exhorting them as to faithfulness and he succeeded in getting them "profess unwavering attachment" to the Methodist Church. Satisfied that he had stymied Baraga's conversion campaign, Pitezel set out on the return journey to his mission. Two painful days of travel later found him huddled in the snow, unable to walk any further.

Pitezel had just finished making his camp when "the priest" arrived en route to Grand Island. Pitezel notified Baraga that he was wasting his time, that the Indians did not want to see him. Nevertheless, Baraga, sometimes known as "the snowshoe priest," continued on his course.

Pitezel's Indian companions treated his ailment in their traditional manner by lacerating his ankle with a sharp flint and rubbing in liniment. Finding his ankle somewhat improved the next morning he set out, following the path through the drifts Baraga had broken. Pitezel's lameness soon returned. But he pushed on by using his string device to raise his snowshoe, making as many as 35 painful miles a day.

Two weeks after he had left his mission, Pitezel limped up to his family, having traveled 240 miles on snowshoes. Although Pitezel considered that ordeal

The Rev. John Pitezel's book included on illustration of Horseshoe Harbor near Copper Harbor at the tip of the Keewenaw Peninsula.

"one of the most laborious and painful journeys of my life," he thought it well worth the effort. Years later he had the satisfaction of seeing Chief Monomonee and his family settled at the mission at Naomikong Point on Whitefish Bay, "firmly attached to Protestant Christianity and constant worshippers with us."

Pitezel remained three years at the Kewawenon Mission. From it which he often made wide ranging journeys on foot, snowshoe and canoe to the outlying missions. His next assignment was among the "godless miners" at Eagle River. Used to the peace and solitude of his Indian missions, Pitezel found the incessant noise of the mining community "a constant annoying din," more than even a "shouting Methodist" preacher could bear. He wrote:

"Bells ring for shift changes, men talk, cars rumble, minerals drop,and six ponderous steam stampers work all night. Machinery whines and the blasts of explosions are heard. And the mules in a nearby barn fight."

In 1848, the Michigan Annual Methodist Conference appointed Pitezel superintendent of the entire Indian Mission District. From his new headquarters at Sault Ste Marie, where, incidently, he found "the moral soil cold and sterile," Pitezel periodically inspected his far flung missions. In his spare time he ministered to the spiritual needs of the wild and wooly village couched at the St. Marys Rapids.

During the summer of 1852, a few months before Pitezel was transferred to a new assignment in Kalamazoo, he held the first Methodist camp meeting in the Upper Peninsula, a gala week long festival at Whitefish Point attended by hundreds of Indians. There the Chippewa adopted Pitezel into the tribe and presented him with his Indian name, *Wa-zah-wah-wa-doong*, the Yellow Bear.

Pitezel proudly included his Indian appellation on

the title page of his narrative of experiences in the Upper Peninsula. The volume proved popular, running through four editions in five years. A revised edition issued in 1882 contains a supplemental chapter detailing some subsequent events.

In 1859 Pitezel authored a juvenile version of his life, *The Backwoods Boy Who Became a Preacher*, and two years later a religious tract, *Stray Leaves from the Budget of an Itinerant*. Both of these volumes have mercifully been forgotten. Pitezels first book, however, remains a prime source for documenting the history of the Upper Peninsula during one of its most colorful eras.

Pitezel, who had grown up in Tiffin City, Ohio, died at the age of 92 in 1906. The memory of the zealous Methodist missionary is not perpetuated in any Michigan placename. That of his Catholic nemesis, however, lives on in the community of Baraga, Baraga County and Baraga State Park.

The Junction

There's a little hotel run by Orson Dunham at the Junction - lots of curves, you bet, even more, when you get - to the Junction. Although stage coach passengers traveling between Kalamazoo and Grand Rapids in the 1850s may not have sung those lyrics - even if they knew the words the plank road was far to bumpy for harmony - one thing is certain. The Junction referred to, and which we now know as Plainwell, was a welcome landmark to many a jolt-weary traveler.

Prior to 1852 Plainwell differed little from the other farm lands of Gun Plains Township. But events were taking place in Kalamazoo and Grand Rapids that would change all that. The plank road that would connect those cities and a spur to Allegan was "acomin." The intersection of that spur, the junction, soon developed into a lively commercial center.

The story actually begins with Michigan's dreadful roads, even the best of which were next to impassible in the spring. Following its stormy entrance into the Union in 1837, the state had launched an ambitious "internal improvements" program that featured numerous railroads, canals and highways. But the hard times triggered by the Panic of 1837 brought the state to the verge of bankruptcy and the various transportation projects ground to a halt. The Michigan Southern and the Michigan Central railroads passed into private hands. By 1846 the latter had snaked its way to Kalamazoo. Both lines reached Chicago six years later, to provide excellent shipping facilities for communities through which they passed. Grand Rapids, however, lay some 30 miles north of the nearest rails.

In addition, little if nothing had been done by the state government to upgrade Michigan's notoriously wretched roads. If anything was to be accomplished it appeared to be up to private enterprise. Consequently the State Legislature granted charters to numerous plank road companies.

The Kalamazoo and Grand Rapids Plank Road Company began soliciting subscriptions in the summer of 1849. By that fall it had begun acquiring planks, surveying the route and securing the right of way. Two years later, the company had raised $37,000 and under the vigorous direction of Charles Shepard and William Withey of Grand Rapids and Israel Kellogg and former Governor Epaphroditus Ransom of Kalamazoo construction commenced.

Plank roads were normally constructed of eight to 16 feet long, four inch thick pine or oak boards laid across wooden stringers. When new they offered a smooth and easy ride.

By the summer of 1855 the entire 48 mile length of the Grand Rapids and Kalamazoo Plank Road, covering a course now known as old U.S. 131, or Douglass Avenue, had been completed. Travelers paid tolls ranging from one cent per mile for a horse and rider to two cents per mile for a wagon drawn by two horses at toll houses located at 12 mile intervals. That is, unless they veered off at "shunpikes," as the short stretches of road that bypassed the toll gates were called.

The first entrepreneur to recognize the commercial possibilities of the junction of the Allegan spur of the plank road was Henry Wellever. He purchased an acre there and began construction of a hotel in the fall of 1853. Then along came Orson D. Dunham from Eaton Rapids who acquired the 40 acres surrounding the Junction. Soon he bought out Wellever. Dunham finished the hotel that was later named the Plainwell House, and in July, 1854, it opened "as a place of entertainment for wearied, hungry men and beasts." Patterson, Glenn & Lyon's

In 1869 when the Junction became Plainwell its downtown looked like this.

Stage Coach Line utilized the hotel as a stop over point as a well as a terminal for passengers headed for Allegan.

By 1855, the Junction had grown to encompass a general store, shoemaker shop, blacksmith shop, schoolhouse, and a dozen or more dwellings. Five years later some 200 people called the Junction home. Many found employment at the newly constructed rake factory, grist mill and planning mill. In short, the Junction had became a boom town. In 1868, when the Lake Shore and Michigan Southern Railroad reached the Junction, the bustling community numbered nearly 1,000 residents and it sported a bank and newspaper.

It was high time, civic leaders decided, to recognize the fact that the community was no longer merely the Junction. Accordingly, on March 26, 1869, it incorporated as a village. The first choice for a name, Plainfield, had unfortunately already been awarded by the Post Office Department to a Livingston County hamlet. Instead, Junctionites became Plainwellians.

It was about that time that the railroad also reached Grand Rapids. The plank road which had served as the city's "principal and very serviceable avenue of communication for business, for passengers and for freight" fell on bad times. The company failed to maintain the plank road properly. Rotted and missing planks reduced the once fine road to "an enlarged washboard."

Asa H. Stoddard, the "farmer poet" from nearby Cooper, the next station on the plank road to the east, published in 1880 a poetic description of what a ride on the plank had been reduced:

"Wagons creaking, groaning, cracking,
Wrecks bestrewing either bank,
Jarring, jolting, jambing, dashing

This is riding on the Plank."
Crocks and baskets rolling, smashing,
Helpless owners looking blank,
Eggs and butter mixing, mashing,
Cannot help it on the Plank.

During a lecture tour to Grand Rapids in the 1870s Mark Twain also experienced a ride on the Kalamazoo and Grand Rapids Plank Road. When someone thought to ask how he liked his trip, the humorist replied, "It would have been good if some unconscionable scoundrel had not now and then dropped a plank across it." It is a pity no one asked him what he thought of the prosperous community that had grown up at the Junction - the proud"Island City" of today.

Puddleford and Its People

Pioneer Constantine, which began its existence as Meek's Mill in 1828, contributed more than its fair share of prominent Michiganders. John Stuart Barry settled in the little community on the St. Joseph River in 1834 and established a general store and riverboat operation that earned him a tidy fortune. Among other political honors, Barry won election as governor of Michigan in 1842, 1846 and 1850.

Affable John J. Bagley, the Detroit tobacco tycoon, spent his childhood years from 1840-1846 in Constantine. He would also serve as governor, winning election by a large majority in 1872.

Joseph R. Williams, another Constantine resident active in state politics, was offered the option of receiving the Republican nomination for governor in 1857 or of becoming president of the newly created Michigan Agricultural College. He choose the latter and guided the East Lansing institution through its tough formative years.

Yet another politico from pioneer-era Constantine and a friend of Barry's, the Hon. Henry H. Riley, lawyer, prosecuting attorney and state senator, won national fame for his literary accomplishments. His *Puddleford Papers*, set in Constantine and filled with thinly veiled characterizations of local personalities, entertained generations of 19th century readers. With rare humor and satire Riley depicted the rough and tumble life on the Michigan frontier. Boisterous, opinionated, crude and vulgar, yet lovable, the characters that people the pages of the *Puddleford Papers* deserve a better fate than to be forgotten. Though long out of print Riley's work is well worth reading for an intimate view of the Michigan that once was.

Consider, for example, Riley's description of a dance held at Bulliphant's Eagle Tavern:

107

Now and then the country quality held a regular blow-out at Bulliphant's tavern. On these occasions, dancing commenced at two in the afternoon, and ended at daylight next morning. Dry goods and perfumery suffered about those days. The girls and boys dressed their hair with oil of cinnamon and wintergreen, and the Eagle smelt like an essence shop. It fairly over powered the stench of Bulliphant's whiskey-bottles. Every one rigged out to within an inch of their lives. The girls wore ruffles on their pantalets frizzled down over their shoes, nearly concealing the whole foot; and all kinds and colors of ribbons streamed from their heads and waists. The "boys" mounted shirt-collars without regard to expense, and flaunted out their brass breast-pins, two or more to each, with several feet of watch-chain jingling in front. The landlord of the Eagle termed these gatherings his "winter harvest."

In another delightful chapter, Riley captured Constantine's combat with that scourge of pioneer life, the ague. Characterized by debilitating periods of fever and chills the disease is now recognized as malaria carried by the hordes of mosquitos that bred in Michigan swamps. But medical authorities of Riley's time had diverse and imaginative theories to account for the spred of the ailment. Riley described the differing opinions of two local doctors concerning the ague's prevalence:

Dr. Dobbs said "that his appearance must be accounted for in this wise - that the marshes were all covered wtih water in the spring, that the sun began to grow so all-fir'd hot long 'bout July and August, that it cream'd over the water with a green scum, and rotted the grass, and this all got stewed inter a morning fog, that rose up and elated itself among the Ox-er-gin and Hy-der-gin, and pizened every body it touched."

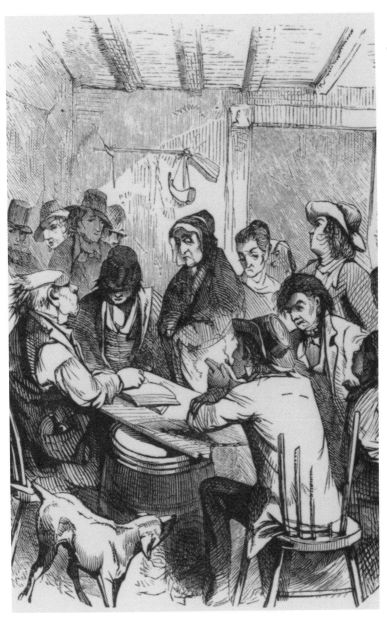

The Hon. Henry H. Riley's book about Constantine
included an illustration of a Justice Court in Puddleford.

Dr. Dobbs delivered this opinion at the public house, in a very oracular style. I noticed several Puddlefordians in his presence at the time, and before he closed, their jaws dropped, and their gaping mouths and expanded eyes were fixed upon him with wonder.

Dr. Teazle declared that "Dobbs didn't know any thing about it. He said the ager was buried up in the airth, and that when the sile was turned up, it got loose, and folks breath'd it into their lungs and from the lungs it went into the liver, and from the liver it went to the kidneys, and the secretions got fuzzled up, and the bile turn'd black, and the blood didn't run, and it set everybody's inards all a-tremblin."

Riley was not the first author to lampoon the crude ways of Michigan's frontier folk. In 1839, Caroline Kirkland, a sophistcated lady from New York, had penned *A New Home Who'll Follow*, a humorous account of her experiences in pioneer Pinckney. But when copies of the volume reached the frontier community and residents recognized themselves it its pages she soon became *persona non grata* there. Eventually she and her family retreated back to New York.

Constantine citizens, evidently, cultivated a better sense of humor. Perhaps, also, Riley tempered his criticisms with an understanding that Kirkland lacked. He wrote: "Puddleford is a great looking-glass, which reflects the faces of almost every person who looks into it, and proves what that remarkable character said, 'that human nature is always the same."

Although residents undoubtedly also recognized themselves and local lore has it that copies of Riley's book with the true names of his charaters identified in manuscript once circulated there, unlike Kirkland, Riley was not banished from village society.

He continued to live in Constantine, a respected member of the community until his death in 1888.

Born in Great Barrington, Mass. on September 1, 1813, Riley was orphaned at the age of ten. He then lived with an uncle in New Hartford, New York, until 1830, when he began an apprenticeship in a Hudson, New York, newspaper office. Four years later he started as a journeyman printer in New York City. For five years beginning in 1837, Riley edited his own paper at Waterloo, New York, and in his spare time he studied the law there.

In 1842, "Michigania" beckoned. Riley sold his newspaper and moved to Kalamazoo, where he "read law" in the office of Nathaniel A. Balch, an early president of Kalamazoo College and later a state senator. After six months study, Riley was admitted to the Michigan bar. He immediately relocated to Constantine where he hung out his shingle. A Democrat, Riley served as prosecuting attorney for St. Joseph County for four years begining in 1846, as a state senator in 1850 and 1862 and as a commissioner to the State Constitutional Convention of 1873. He gained "a very high reputation as a well-read lawyer, a good pleader, and a safe counselor."

As Riley carved out his career as a lawyer he continued to gather information which he would utilize in his regional fiction pieces. Some of the most memorable characters in his book, in fact, are members of the legal profession, including a rascally Judge Roy Bean type character named Squire Jonathan Longbow and pettifoggers Ike Turtle and Sile Bates.

In the early 1850s Riley first tried his Puddleford stories on the public's palate in the pages of the *Knickerbocker Magazine,* at that time one of the nation's leading monthlies. The popularity of his articles led him to assemble them in book form in 1854 as *Puddleford and Its People.* Another edition appeared two years later under a New York imprint as

The Puddleford Papers or Humors of the West.
In 1875, Riley published an illustrated third revision of *Puddleford* in 1875, the most commonly encountered edition, and his book remained in print at least as late as 1888.

Riley, also maintained an active interest in Michigan history, serving as vice president of the State Pioneer Society and representing that organization at the semi-centennial celebration of statehood in 1887. Prior to his death at his Constantine home the following year, Riley also wrote a series of historical articles on topics ranging from the mound builders in Michigan to the life of his Constantine friend, John S. Barry.

Why no enterprising publisher has put Riley's colorful account of pioneer Constantine back in print remains a mystery. New generations of readers deserve the opportunity to meet Venison Styles, frontiersmen; old Aunt Graves, the Rev. Bigelow Van Slyck, Jim Buzzard and the cast of other unique characters whose vernacular and exploits enliven the pages of this midwestern frontier classic.

"Thou Shall Not Covet Thy Neighbor's Ox"

They were "bright red, long, large and gentle looking fellows, as near alike as two peas." Yes sir, Leander S. Prouty's team of two-year-old steers was as superb a pair of oxen as could be found in the whole of Allegan County maybe even the state. Prouty, Allegan's original settler and the first to permanently locate in neighboring Trowbridge Township, proudly hawed and geed his team around the second annual Allegan County Fair in 1854.

Unfortunately, in the process the oxen rubbed off their identification labels and as a result they were "passed by" for the award they so clearly deserved. First prize for the best working oxen went instead to John Clifford, another Trowbridge Township pioneer, who also happened to be on the judging committee.

The historical record fails to document whether that incident brought hard feelings between the two old pioneers, but one thing is certain - oxen, or working cattle, were serious business in 1854.

The state census taker counted 67,033 of them that year - 1,286 in Allegan County alone. Compared to only 851 horses in the county, oxen were clearly the prime source of muscle on the farms then being carved from the wilderness.

Pioneers favored oxen over their equine counterparts for a number of good reasons. They were cheaper to obtain - bull calves converted to steers were worth far less than cows or horses. They were also cheaper to feed since they thrived on pasture and hay while working horses needed grain. Leather horse harnesses were expensive and wore out while a simple wooden ox yoke lasted almost indefinitely. Horses were subject to more diseases and easily hurt themselves among stumpy fields. Steers were as "strong as an ox" and tougher and easier to manage in tight situations. Last but not least, when they grew old or times got tough oxen could be slaughtered and eaten.

The major disadvantages lay in the fact that most were "slow as an ox" "stubborn as an ox," and "dumb as an ox." Furthermore they could not be ridden and a brace of oxen lacked the prestige of a horse team. While it was a rare frontiersman who could not guide a team of horses, a pioneer maxim held "a man may be able to govern men and guide the state and yet make a poor fist of it in holding a breaking plow behind seven or eight yoke of oxen."

The power of the beasts worshipped by the ancient Egyptians in honor of Apis, the god who taught them the art of husbandry, was proverbial. John Adams, who pioneered in Lenawee County in 1831, recalled breaking up a virgin field with hazel brush growing on it taller than a man using an ox drawn plow. He testified: "They cut a strip about 20 inches in width, six to eight inches deep, turning brush under and covering it just as an ordinary plow would turn under corn stalks or weeds."

Another Lenawee County pioneer, Andrew Howell, reminisced:

For a considerable time a horse was rarely seen in the township. The ox team was the great reliance of the settler. With it he did his logging and teaming on the road, and in summer, before sufficient land was cleared for pasture, when the day's work was over, the oxen were turned out into the woods to graze, with great bells strapped to their necks, so they might be found when needed.

The early records of Allegan County also contain many references to the importance of oxen. Dr. Samuel Foster, the first man to settle at the site of Otsego, traveled via the Erie Canal and Lake Erie to

114

A typical Michigan scene in 1855 included a plowman hawing and geeing his ox team.

Detroit in 1831. There he bought a yoke of oxen, loaded his goods and family on a covered wagon, and the pioneers slowly plodded their way across the state on the miserable roads then in existence. Oxen, incidently, did a better job in the mud than horses. Tarrying briefly at Battle Creek where he made a little money erecting the first two log cabins at that site, he eventually reached his new homesite on the south bank of the Kalamazoo River by fall. The log house he built there "became the rallying point for all important meetings of the early pioneers and he was one of Otsego's most prominent citizens."

Similarly, Justus B. Sutherland also purchased a yoke of oxen and a wagon in Detroit in 1834, packed his wife and six children on board and started for his new home in the wilderness of Allegan County's Gun Plains Township. It took him five days to reach Gull Prairie in Kalamazoo County. The streams he crossed enroute were bridged only by floating logs, "which often rolled under the oxen's feet, looking at times as though a ducking, if nothing worse, awaited the whole family." But the Sutherlands made it to Gun Plains Township unscathed and with the help of their ox team began converting the wilderness into a prize farm. A half century later Sutherland was considered "a man respected and esteemed by all who know him."

In 1847, Mr. and Mrs. Roswell Rockwell "made their weary way in a lumber wagon surrounded by their six children and all their worldly effects" from Seneca County, Ohio, to Trowbridge Township. Rockwell shrewdly traded his team of horses to one of the Dutch immigrants then flocking to the northwestern section of Allegan County for a yoke of oxen and a quantity of gold pieces. The oxen proved better for his purposes and the gold provided the down payment on his farm. It is not recorded how the Hollander made out with the horses.

Oxen were indispensable to the pioneers in conveying them through the wilderness, plowing unbroken land, snaking out tree trunks and many other uses. What's more "close association with oxen undoubtedly contributed in no small part to the patience and perseverance of frontier people."

The frontier line could be plotted by the relative percentage of working cattle and horses. Once the wilderness had been subdued, oxen also soon went "under the axe." The number of oxen in Michigan reached a peak in 1854, dropping each decade until by 1940 only 75 yoke remained in remote sections of the state. One additional reason for their demise was articulated that year by S.B. Cudney, an 85-year-old master ox driver from Charlotte: "the man who never was kicked by an ox never drove oxen."

A few show ox teams remain in Michigan and the Kalamazoo based Tillers International Organization maintains a working ox team to demonstrate its potential for use in developing countries. But for the most part we are left only with historical refereces and, of course, the tenth commandment: "Thou shalt not covet thy neighbor's house... nor his ox."

Grandma Moulton Remembers

The fireplace cast a ruddy glow on the old woman, lending color to her pale features and tingeing her white hair once again with auburn. An occasional pop from the fire punctuated the rhythmic squeak of her sewing rocker and the click of knitting needles.

At her feet sat the girl she had once been, dark eyes dancing with excitement.

"Grandma, please tell me another story," she pleaded.

"Oh mercy me, I was just thinking of your grandpa. You know its been, let me see now," she paused to compute, "60 - yes 60 years since he stood there so straight and tall in his blue army uniform. I'll tell you about how your Grandpa Belah Moulton joined the Union Army."

"Now you remember, I was younger than your grandpa. I was born in Cherry Valley, New York, on May 4, 1851. When I was four years old my father brought me to Allegan County, to Otsego, where he had a job teaching school. I lived there and on a farm near Martin Corners, what they now call simply Martin, for the next 16 years."

"Your grandpa was 11-years-old when he moved with his family from Jefferson County, New York, to Martin Township in 1857. He was a large boy for his age and a good worker. His father, who had the same name as he did, was a strict Methodist and he believed that boys should work hard on the farm because idleness was the devil's tool."

"Even though he was five years older than me, we became childhood chums. My father, Cortland B. Smith, lived on a farm about a mile and a half from the Moulton homestead. So we both attended the same country school where my father was the school teacher."

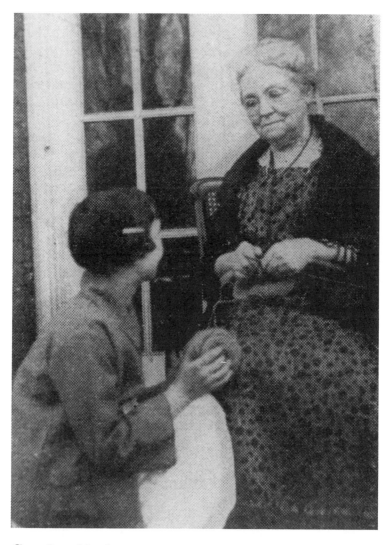

Grandma Moulton told her granddaughter of her pioneer life in Michigan.

"But I'm getting away from my story about your grandpa joining the army. The Civil War broke out in April, 1861. It was all anybody could talk about. How those rebels were defying our constitution and breaking up the Union just so they could keep black folks as slaves."

"Well, there was a big Fourth of July celebration at Martin Corners that first year of the war. Hundreds of people flocked to the town to hear the program. Somebody read the Declaration of Independence in a stirring voice and we all sang the hymn 'America.' There was a big banquet that cost 25 cents a plate and the proceeds paid for the fireworks that blazed across the sky that evening."

"But the main feature of the day was a patriotic address intended to inspire the young men to join the army. There were lots of women, including your grandma, crying our eyes out - we felt so patriotic and noble. Your grandpa Belah was only 15 years old and his brother, Irwin, a year older, but they both decided to lie about their age and enlist in the army to defend their country."

'But they knew their father needed them on the farm and would not give his permission to go. So the following Sunday Belah and Irwin stayed overnight at the home of some neighbor boys who had also decided to run away to be soldiers. Irwin changed his mind, though, and went home and the next morning Mr. Moulton forced him to confess about Belah's plan."

"In the meantime, Belah and the other boys had started to walk along the plank road to Kalamazoo, 20 miles to the south. They had gotten about 15 miles, when your great-grandpa rode up behind them with a big horse whip in his hand. He ordered them to return home on the plank road, while he took a parallel dirt road to avoid paying the penny a mile toll that was charged for a horse and rider."

"The other boys, who had gotten pretty tired of walking by then, returned to their homes. But as soon as your great-grandfather was out of sight, Belah took a road that led southwest. He got meals at farmhouses along the way and slept in hay mounds until a couple of days later he arrived in Paw Paw. From there, somehow, he reached Chicago."

"He worked for a farmer for a few months, then, that fall he enlisted in an Illinois infantry regiment. In the meantime, wouldn't you know it, but the son of the farmer he had worked for got a job teaching school at Martin Corners. He told your great-grandpa about Belah's whereabouts. So Mr. Moulton headed down to Illinois and got a writ of habeas corpus and went to the army camp where your grandpa was in training. Stepping up behind Belah, he tapped him on the shoulder and said, "You are my prisoner.""

"There was nothing your grandpa could do but to go back to Michigan. There he was, back at the drudgery of farm work after all his exciting experiences. But he made up his mind that as soon as he was 16, he would join the army again."

"He got his chance in February, 1864, when a recruiting officer came to Martin Corners. He enlisted as one of the 400 recruits who filled the ranks of the 13th Michigan Infantry in place of those that had been killed. He went down south to Lookout Mountain, Tennessee, for his training. He first saw action against Gen. Nathan Bedford Forrest's fierce cavalrymen.

"That November his regiment joined Gen. Sherman's army and they took part in his great march through Georgia to the sea. He suffered many hardships during that and later campaigns. His uniform grew ragged, his boots wore out and he often didn't have enough to eat. But those soldiers always had plenty of tobacco down South and it was then that your grandpa learned to chew the vile stuff."

"Despite that nasty habit, when he came back to Martin Corners after the war ended in 1865 and he asked me to marry him, I said, yes, even though I was only 16-years-old. Four years went by, as he saved his money to get us well started in life together, before I married that handsome soldier boy. In the spring of 1872 your father was born."

"I'll tell you some more stories about the old days, when your grandpa was alive, some other time. Right now your grandma wants to look into that cheery fireplace and remember to herself how happy your grandpa and I were as we faced the world together all those many years ago."

The "Otsego Vision" That Inspired Cornflakes

"Glory! Glory! Glory!" The words reverberated through Aaron and Lydia Hilliard's little farmhouse located about two miles southwest of the Allegan County community of Otsego.

Startled, the Seventh-day Adventist stalwarts who knelt in the kitchen in prayer gaped in amazement at Ellen G. White. Eyes staring into space, not breathing, arms moving rhythmically with what she saw, the 35-year-old prophetess had been "taken off" in vision.

And what she saw as a result, that evening on June 6, 1863, would determine the future of the Adventist church and indirectly America's eating habits.

The Adventist church traces its origins to the Millerite movement of the 1840s. William Miller, an upstate New York farmer, had applied some esoteric mathematics to the bibical books of Daniel and Revelations and thereby calculated the exact date of Judgment Day - March 21, 1844.

As the fatal day drew near, tens of thousands of his followers donned long white ascension robes, climbed nearby hilltops and gathered in country cemetaries for the graves to open and the heavenly judgement of the quick and the dead. Somehow the church survived that first "great disappointment."

Miller recalculated and came up an alternate date of Oct. 22, 1844, and once again the Millerites let their earthly affairs slide in preparation for the millenium. Some grew hysterical in their anxiety for the world to come. They danced the holy dance and laughed the holy laugh.

That second "great disappointment" and the tar and feather parties staged by non-believers pretty

Ellen G. White received her 1863 "vision" at the Hillard house near Otsego,

well finished off Miller's credibility. Nevertheless, a coterie of diehards kept up their faith that the end was near.

One of those adamant believers was a 17-year-old invalid from Portland, Maine, named Ellen G. Harmon. A few months after the dispersal of the Millerites she began experiencing strange visions that she interpreted as divine communication. Bolstered by those prophetic visions and augmented by the belief that Saturday ought to be observed as the Sabbath, the Seventh-day Adventist Church evolved out of the wreckage of the Millerite movement.

Harmon married another Adventist activist, James White, and together they toured New England and the west preaching the fundamentalist doctrines that they and other church elders had promulgated.

Believing firmly in the power of the press, by 1848 the Whites had begun publishing a denominational journal and various tracts. In 1855 the press relocated from Rochester, New York, to Battle Creek, Michigan, and soon thereafter that city became the church's world headquarters.

White's periodic visions, published and widely disseminated in the form of pamphlets known as testimonials, set church dogma. In other words, White's dreams had clout. Believers, for example, pointed to her vision of January 12, 1861, at Parkville, Michigan, that prophesied the Civil War that would rend the nation three months later.

It was a tent revival held in Otsego by Adventist crusaders R.J. Lawrence and M.E. Cornell that brought Ellen White to that fair city of approximately 1,000 souls in June of 1863. The Whites had mounted a carriage at their home in Battle Creek on the morning of June 6, and bumped over the 30 some dusty miles to Otsego. They planned to spend the night with the Hilliard family, pioneer Otsego Township Adventists.

The Hilliards and their guests had finished supper and knelt down for evening prayers when the vision struck. Forty-five minutes later, White come out of it, gasping for breath - she apparently had not breathed during the entire trance - and muttered the words "Dark, dark."

Pale and limp from her ordeal, White soon retired for the night. But the next day she began to record the wonderful wisdom she had received. By 1864, a testimonial based on what became known as "the Otsego Vision" first instructed the Adventist flock on a new healthier way of life.

Animal flesh was forbidden because, among other things, eating meat strengthened the "animal propensities" which, in turn, created a craving for alcoholic beverages. Salt, spices, sugar, tea, coffee and vinegar, and most other condiments that added zest to the meal were taboo. Tobacco, suspected even then of causing cancer and other diseases, would no longer pollute Adventist breaths. Instead White's followers would dine on fruits, vegetables, grains and nuts, all washed down with hearty draughts of tepid water.

The Otsego Vision also laid the foundation for the Adventist health spa established as the Western Health Reform Institute in Battle Creek three years later. There ailing Adventists and others were treated to various "hydropathic" procedures which relied on the medical effects of copious quantites of cold water inside and out and a diet of rock hard graham flour "gems." That establishment languished, however, until in 1876, a young Adventist doctor and one of the White's proteges, John Harvey Kellogg, took over its management.

Kellogg, a flamboyant and brilliant entrepreneur, renamed the institute the Battle Creek Sanitarium, (a word he made up) reorganized the regimen to make it a bit more "user friendly" and began a building campaign. Thanks to his genius for promotion and medical acumen the "San" soon became a household word across America.

Kellogg also introduced a variety of health foods that offered tastier alternatives to the bland vegetarian diet. Over the years he invented granola, peanut butter, protose and nuttolene (meat substitutes) and caramel cereal coffee. During the 1890s he teamed up with younger brother W.K. Kellogg to give the world its first flaked breakfast cereals..

Following a brief stay at the "San," a dyspepic Texan named Charles W. Post parlayed what he had learned there into a multi-million dollar industry. His Grape Nuts, Post Toasties and the corn flakes and other ready-to-eat breakfast foods manufactured by the W.K. Kellogg Company revolutionized the American breakfast table and ultimately freed housewives to do better things with their time than cook elaborate and greasy morning meals.

And it all began with a vision experienced by Ellen G. White in a rural Otsego farmhouse.

Quad's Odds

Charles B. Lewis, Michigan's most successful 19th Century humorist, launched his literary career with a bang - the explosion of a steam boiler that is. In 1868 Lewis left his position as typesetter for the Lansing *State Democrat* to accept a better job with the Maysville, Kentucky, *Bulletin*. Boarding a steamboat at Cincinnati, he embarked on what he thought would be a leisurely trip up the Ohio River.

Lewis described what happened next in his humorous article, "Up Among the Splinters:"

After the steamer left the wharf-boat I sat down in the cabin and listened with others, while a fat man from Illinois read four or five columns of the impeachment trial of Andy Johnson. Throwing the paper down he said:
"Gentlemen, it seems to me ...."
He stopped right there. He couldn't go on. The boilers exploded just then, and we had business aloft. I don't exactly remember who went up first, or how we got throught the roof. I am a little absent-minded sometimes, and this was one of the times.
The boilers made a great deal more noise than there seemed any occasion for. The explosion would have been A-1 with half the whizzing, grinding and tearing. One of the men who came up behind me seemed to think that something or other was out of order, and he yelled out to me:
"Say! What's all this?"
I pointed to the fat man, who was about five feet ahead of me, and than I began to practice gymnastics. I went up a few feet right end up then a few feet more wrong end up, and then I wasn't particular about which way I went up...

We finally arrived there. It was a good ways up, and the route had several little inconveniences. It was a grand location from which to view the surrounding country, but we didn't stop to view it. We had business below, and our motto was business before pleasure."

Lewis survived his ensuing plunge into the river by clinging to wreckage from the boat. But the fat man and several others did not. Burned and battered, the young newspaperman lay close to death in a Cincinnati hospital for three months before returning to Lansing. He concluded his article about his near fatal experience by observing: "It isn't good to be blown up. There are better ways of ascending and descending. Such things interrupt traveling programs, and are often the foundation of funeral processions."

Back at his old job on the Lansing newspaper, Lewis composed his facetious account of being blown up directly into type. The editor published it under the pseudonym his typesetter chose, M. Quad, actually a measurement used in setting type. Widely reprinted in other papers, it soon made "the whole West burst into laughter." Among those laughing at Lewis' first and succeeding sketches was the editor of the Detroit *Free Press* who lured him to join his staff at the "City of the Straits."

Lewis' daily sketches published in the *Free Press* met with a wide popular following. Within a few years he invented a number of distinctive characters who figured in his stories, including a droll judge of a Detroit police court named "His Honor" and Brother Gardner, a witty black gentlemen who presided over the Lime Kiln Club.

In an 1886 article about Detroit published in *Harper's Monthly* Edmund Kirke labled Lewis "perhaps the most unique and genuine humorist this

Humorist Charles B. Lewis included a fanciful depiction of a Detroit court scene in his 1875 book.

country has produced..." Kirke wrote that "humor gushes from him like champagne from an uncorked bottle, bubbling and effusive, and drenching us, whether we will or not, with laughter. And there is wisdom with his wit - strong, homely common-sense mixed with a racy, unctuous humor which makes his wisdom as grateful to our taste as whale oil is to the palate of an Esquimau."

Credited by Kirke and others as one of the factors behind the rapid increase in circulation of the *Free Press*, particularly its London edition, Lewis' popularity brought him an annual salary of $10,000 during an era when male factory workers often brought home less than $10.00 for a 55 hour work week. Despite Lewis' large public following, Edward G. Holden, a fellow member of the *Free Press* staff during the 1870s and 1880s, remembered him as "not a specially agreeable or popular person among his co-workers" whom he twitted about the smallness of their salaries compared with his own.

Born in Liverpool, Ohio, in 1842, Lewis moved to Lansing with his family at the age of 12. George P. Sanford, a young schoolteacher who arrived in the capitol city two years later, recalled that "Charley Lewis kept the school in a roar with his funny declarations." Following graduation Lewis attended the Michigan Agricultural College in 1857 and 1858.

When the Civil War broke out, the 19-year-old Lewis answered. "Father Abram's" call, enlisting in the Third Michigan Infantry at Grand Rapids in May, 1861. His first tour of duty ended prematurely, however, when he was discharged for disability the following September. By February, 1865, he had evidently recovered enough to enlist again in the Sixth Michigan Cavalry at Jackson. Later transferred to the First Michigan Cavalry, he was among those sent west to fight Indians after the war was over, finally receiving his discharge at Fort Leavenworth in

February, 1866.

Lewis took advantage of his newspaper popularity to compile his first book in 1875. A 480 page collection of humorous pieces and moral and temperance sketches that combined satire with pathos, *Quad's Odds* reprinted some of the best of his newspaper articles with additional material. Published by the *Free Press*, and illustrated by L.H. Crumb in a manner reminiscent of some of Samuel Clemens' contemporary volumes, the handsome book, "each copy guaranteed full weight," sold well.

The compilation opened with the story that first won Lewis fame "Up Among the Splinters." Portions of the book, particularly Lewis' temperance propaganda, is hardly worth persuing today. Modern readers may not understand certain aspects of his humor and some dated references. Nevertheless, much remains that will reward reading and chuckling over, including numerous scenarios inspired by Lewis' Michigan experiences.

Any writer who has suffered mangled prose at the hands of an inept copy editor, known as proof readers in Lewis' day, will appreciate his humorous litany of wrongs they had inflicted on his work and his final malediction;

May no tailor trust him! May all dogs bite him! May he sink with an ocean steamer, get scorched in a prairie fire, or go down with some falling bridge. Every village board and city council should pass an ordinance making it a misdemeanor for any person to harbor a proof-reader over night. They never die. They grow old until they reach a certain point, and then they stick right there. Nothing ever throws them out of a situation. They go on year after year, killing editors and reporters by inches, and there is no law to prevent. If they get consumption they still live. If they fall down stairs they do not break a bone. If they become blind they go right on reading proof and putting in "Dick and Kate" for the fairly written "delicate."

Sadly, in 1891 Lewis left the state that had catapulted him to fame, seeking greener pastures in New York where he wrote for the *World*. Ultimately he settled in Brooklyn. Prior to his death in 1924 Lewis authored several additional volumes including *Brother Gardner's Lime Kiln Club* (1894), based on other of his *Free Press* articles, *The Life and Troubles of Mr. Bowser* (1902) and a collection of Civil War articles. Whether Lewis found greater happiness in the "Big Apple" is open to conjecture. Perhaps he should have followed the conclusion he reached in an article in *Quad's Odds* about the hypocrasy of tomb stone epitaphs:

I found Deacon Warner's tombstone also. It bears a stern, solemn look, just as he used to, and it says: "Heaven's gates shall open to us who are like him."
Perhaps they will. Whether they do or not, I shall always remember how he sold me a blind horse when I had sore eyes; how he raised house rent on the widows; how a Justice fined him twenty-five dollars for thrashing a poor bound-boy; how he put chicory in his coffee and hay-seed in his tea, and how regularly he used to pass the contribution box to the rest of us, but forgot to put in anything himself. If the gates of Heaven are going to be held wide open for those of Deacon Warner's class, I want to put in my time in Michigan.

Charles W. Jay:
Oceana County Comic

The Chicago and Michigan Lakeshore Railroad conductor, remembered only "as a gentleman in very thin legs and astonishingly large feet," gazed intently into the eyes of the passenger who had boarded the train in Muskegon that November morning in 1871. Then, shaking his head slightly in pity, passed on without saying a word.

The passenger, concerned at the snail's pace with which the train was negotiating the 16 mile stretch from Muskegon to Whitehall, had, after the elapse of 30 minutes, suggested to the conductor "that he reverse the cow-catcher to the rear of the train, for fear that a drove of cattle, that started for Muskegon a few minutes after we did, might run into us." Charles W. Jay, a homesteader from New Jersey with a well developed sense of humor, had arrived in Michigan. The only question remaining - was Michigan ready for him?

Suddenly quitting his 30 year career as a Trenton, New Jersey, journalist because of some murky political problems, the 56-year-old, who in appearance and mannerisms resembled New York editor Horace Greeley, had decided to follow his look alike's sage advice and "Go West."

Jay would start life anew in the backwoods of Benona Township, Oceana County. His son-in-law, Charles A. Sessions, had purchased a 40 acre tract about a mile and half south of Little Point au Sable in 1867. Prior to moving his family there in 1871 Sessions planted the first large commercial peach orchard in the county. Lured by the prospect of reaping an easy living from those golden fruit Jay bought sight unseen an adjoining 40 acres containing an old tumble down log cabin. While his wife and two children went on ahead to ready the homestead, Jay finished up his affairs in Trenton, leaving for his new home in Northern Michigan several months later.

He traveled to Chicago by rail, which he reached without incident, setting aside the accidental uncoupling of the "palace car" he slept in while the rest of the train continued on for about 20 miles before the engineer discovered the loss. Jay found the charred ruins of Chicago still smoldering from the fiery apocalypse it had suffered a month before. He noted for miles "scarce a wall was left standing, vast heaps of machinery disjointed and warped out of all usefulness and the principal blocks of stores could be traced by the huge iron safes, that still rested, in almost uniform lines where they dropped through into the ashes." After poking around the debris during his five hour layover there Jay left on the train for Milwaukee.

The following evening, in company with 50 lumberjacks heading for jobs in the Michigan pine forests, he scurried aboard the *Belle of the Lake* and steamed across to Grand Haven. Jay awoke at dawn and climbed to the deck for his first glimpse of the glorious state with which he had cast his lot:

The high sandy bluffs of the Michigan shore of the lake loomed up dimly in the far distance. A thousand sea gulls flapped their white wings against the placid waters, or sailed in the higher atmosphere above us. Far inland, out of the majestic forests of green topped hemlock and pine, the crimson heralds of the coming god of day began to kindle their resplendid fires.

Jay boarded a train at Grand Haven for the 15 mile trip to Muskegon. That robust lumber city with a population of more than 6,000 amazed him with its bustling vigor. Yet he noted that "the blackened stumps of the recent wilderness still stand thickly in her principal street."

At Muskegon Jay changed trains for the final railroad leg of his journey - Whitehall, then the end of the line. That slow moving experience was varied only by his repartee with the conductor and another humorous exchange with a train boy hawking items to passengers. Jay asked him for a New York *Tribune*. Having never heard of that famous newspaper, the backwoods youth thought he wanted a New York trombone. Sliding past Jay, the boy joined the conductor in keeping a close eye on the "old feller over thar that's crazy."

Jay found Whitehall laid out on an elevated plain overlooking the White River with a "truly pretty situation." Montague, its twin city across the river, would not be founded for another three years. At Whitehall Jay hired a teamster to drive him the remaining 22 miles to his destination. The eight dollars he paid him represented more than a week's wages by 1870s standards.

During the first 18 miles of their winding journey through the dense overarching hemlock forest they encountered not one sign of mankind. Then they began to hear the sound of the axe ringing in the wilderness as they sighted scattered little clearings. Soon Jay noted "little peach orchards among the blackened stumps, the trees of which had just been set out, and ground was being prepared for others as fast as the axe could dispossess the old forest trees of their freehold."

As they passed along the 360 feet high bluff of the "Clay Banks," a celebrated Indian gathering place and burial ground, Jay enjoyed a spectacular view of Lake Michigan, "its green, limpid waters seem rolled out to immensity." Approximately seven miles north of the Clay Banks, the wagon ascended another high elevation topped with a 40 acre clearing. Jay had arrived at his new home, a site known as Blackberry Ridge because of the profusion of that

Charles W. Jay's log cabin undoubtedly resembled that his Benona Township neighbor, James Gibbs, erected in 1850.

fruit found by early settlers. As he drove up, his children, John and Alice, ran forward in welcome. Hugs and kisses completed, Jay surveyed for the first time his homestead:

I found my domestic fortress in these inhospitable wilds to be a cabin of decayed and crumbling logs, upon whose roof, from the outside, I could "lay hands" without theological authority. But my wife, who is an extravagant and pretentious woman, had "unbeknownst" to me, and without marital authority from the party on the other part, added a $50.00 addition to the north side of our ancient and time honored domicil. This little exhibition of wifely pride and womanly vanity has probably blighted my political aspirations forever and a day. The less favored settlers have booked me in their memories as a "rustikrat" invader upon their simple tastes and habits! I came here with visions of a future seat in Congress; but a woman has let Satin into this paradise of anticipatory salary grabbing."

But even Jay's seemingly inexhaustible sense of humor was pushed to its limits during his first winter in northern Michigan. Two days after his arrival it began snowing - "for six long weeks it continued, with almost unbroken violence, and in all that period the sun was not visible for two hours." Violent winds from the northwest sculpted great drifts of the five feet of snow that fell in December. In mid April Jay nearly perished when caught in a sudden blizzard miles from his cabin. Worse than the weather which imprisoned him in his cabin for weeks at a time seemed the general lack of society. Accustomed to eastern urban amenities Jay found not one single store, tavern or church in all Benona Township. The township also was as dry as the sand-dunes surrounding nearby Silver Lake, without "one drop of ameliorating whiskey for even medical purposes."

Jay survived the solitude of that first winter and when spring finally released him from winter's icy fetters he embraced his agricultural labor as a welcome diversion. He set out a 30 acre orchard with 3,000 peach trees, 1,000 apples, 500 quince and plum and assorted pear, cherry, etc. He seeded six acres in corn, five in navy beans and several other crops. The four acres of "Early Rose" potatoes he planted became his pet crop. While preparing the ground for planting he had, he was convinced, discovered a valuable acquisition to medical science, that "there is some secreted virtue in a Northern Michigan hoe handle, that raises blisters in a few minutes, as large as life, and twice as natural."

His potatoes did well in that virgin sandy soil. And "no fond mother ever watched over the dawning beauty of her first born," Jay recalled, as did he "over the developing glory of them 'taters'." But then, to his maternal dismay, a swarm of potato bugs attacked the field and began devouring the plants. Bitterly depressed, Jay sat on a stump surveying the insects' ravages, when Pete Higgins strode up. Known as "the old settler" because of his 20 year residence in the vicinity, Higgins had taken advantage of Jay's frontier inexperience repeatedly in the past, selling him frozen seed potatoes and borrowing money that he never repaid. Nevertheless, a bond of sorts had grown between the two. Higgins, as usual, was more than happy to share his frontier wisdom:

Why, stranger, you can kill every blasted critter of em, sure as a shootin; before 9 o'clock tomorrow morning. Go and get a bushel of fresh lime, what's just outen the kiln. Pound it up as fine as powder and early in morning; when the dew is thick, dust them are vines all over, and by noon there won't be a durn'd live 'tater bug in the hull patch."

Jay thanked his benefactor profusely for his advice, quickly hitched up his horse, drove the eight miles to the nearest store at Stony Creek, purchased the lime and worked all night pulverizing it into a powder. Early the next morning he dusted his entire patch. As he watched for the results " the dust began to seethe and bubble, and a smoke steamed up, and the vines squirmed and writhed, and soon lay prone upon the ground!"

As Jay solemnly contemplated his ruined crop, Higgins made his appearance again, reminding him in a satisfied tone:

"Well stranger, you see the lime has cleared the kitchen. Bugs all dead, I b'lieve" "Yes," Jay bitterly rejoined, "and vines, too. Did you know it would kill the vines?"

"Why of course I know'd it would kill the 'taters. Any durn'd fool who had the sense he was born with oughter to know that! But then look at the satisfaction of circumventin the cussed bugs!"

Jay, somehow managed to keep his self control and not try to strangle the old settler and, in fact, survived several more such incidents, humorous only in retrospect. He recorded his Oceana County experiences in *My New Home in Northern Michigan and Other Tales,* a 180 page book published back in Trenton in 1874. Jay admitted in the preface to having penned the book for the prospect of making money, an effort to recoup some of his fortune he had lost in the Financial Panic of 1873. Despite that disaster and the loss of his potato crop the year before, Jay survived. The *Oceana County History* published in 1882 noted he had a fine orchard of 5,000 fruit trees and 10,000 blackberry bushes. That volume also corroborated much of the information Jay included in his humorous accounts of frontier life. Prior to his death in 1884, the irrepressible humorist also penned numerous witty articles about the life he led on the Oceana County frontier. They appeared in area newspapers under the penname, O.P. Dildock.

Asa H. Stoddard:
The Farmer Poet

The old farmer chucked to his horse, deftly swung the plow onto its side as the animal circled around and at just the right moment sunk the point back into the field, throwing up an even curl of black Cooper Township soil. It was an era when a man's worth was measured by how straight a furrow he could plow and when the term "he balked in his furrow" meant something. Yes sir, Asa Harding Stoddard was a good farmer and more than that - he was a poet.

On this particular spring morning in the 1870s his mind was on food and he felt a poem coming on. When he got to the end of the next furrow, he gave the horse a breather, pulled a scrap of paper out from under his hat, licked his pencil and leaning against a fence post began to write:

"How sweet to my taste was the bread of my childhood,
That fond recollection recalls to my mind;
When hungry I came, from the school or the wild-wood;
An old-fashioned johnny cake hoping to find."

About that time, the sun overhead and his growling stomach told Stoddard it was time for dinner. He headed for the big brick farm house where he knew wife Laura Jane's kitchen would be fragrant with a rich country meal. Yet he couldn't get that johnny cake, or what some folks call corn bread, out of his mind. Halfway to the house, he stopped again and wrote:

"How nice, from the amply filled plate to reach

141

it,
As piece, after piece, took the road to my
mouth;
There was no other bread could induce me to
leave it,
Though loaded with sweets from the far sunny
South."

Stoddard eventually wrote six more stanzas to
his poem, "The Old Fashioned Johnny Cake." And he
published it along with 49 similar pieces in his volume,
Miscellaneous Poems, printed in Kalamazoo in 1880.
Although few copies of the "Farmer Poet's" book
circulated far from Cooper Township, those of the 200
page volume that survive are coveted for their
picturesque discriptions of 19th Century Michigan
rural life.

Born in Williamson, New York, in 1814,
Stoddard received little in the way of formal education
as a child. He later pilloried in a poem his unfortunate
experiences when he did venture into the one-room
school:

"How feared in my heart were my teachers in
childhood,
As scared recollection recalls them to view;
With their long, ugly whips, that were cut in the
wildwood
That wild, tangled wood where the tough
switches grew."

Nevertheless, at the age of 18 he determined to
become a teacher. He worked that spring and summer
on a local farm for eight dollars a month, saved
enough to buy some decent clothes and attended
school that winter. The following winter he secured a
position as a teacher in a nearby one-room
schoolhouse.

The salary was pitiful and the class consisted of 60 students, some of whom he remembered as "pretty hard cases." Worse yet, he was expected to board around among the various families in the district. Each household was required to provide food and lodging in proportion to the number of students sent to school. One impoverished family that lived in a one room cabin sent seven pupils. While boarding with them, Stoddard slept in a loft in the same bed that was loaded with seven other adults and children. Despite such privations Stoddard enjoyed teaching, and soon won a reputation as an able schoolmaster. He spent the succeeding 24 winters in the classroom.

In the biographical sketches he penned late in life Stoddard recalled that: "At an early age I was much addicted to rhyming." Among his earliest poems were contributions to "young ladies albums." By the time he was 20-years-old he had launched into longer narrative poems. And soon he found himself writing politically oriented pieces in support of the anti-slavery movement, temperance, spiritualism, liberal religion and other causes that appealed to his freethinker's ideology.

But his poetical effusions brought nothing in the way of income and school teacher's wages being what they were in those days, Stoddard continued to farm as well. In 1837, he married one of the students with whose family he had boarded. Tragically, she died of consumption, as tuberculosis was then called, in 1846. Two years later he became engaged to another of his students who seemed healthy enough. But before the marriage she also contracted the dread lung disease. Being a man of his word, he married her anyway in 1848. She died less than a year later. Three years later, having thoroughly investigated her and her family's health history, Stoddard married Laura Jane Sanford. She outlived him by four years, dying at the age of 84 in 1910.

Asa Stoddard's Italianate home appeared in the 1880 Kalamazoo County History.

Stoddard had traveled through Michigan in 1836 while en route to Indiana and 27 years later he pulled up stakes in New York and moved to Kalamazoo County's Cooper Township for good. In 1870 he purchased a 200 acre farm in sections 27 and 34 of Cooper Township along with a partially finished Italianate dwelling. Stoddard finished the house and converted the farm into one of the finest in the township.

Stoddard continued to write his poetry as he grew older, seemingly able to dash off verses in honor of any occasion that came along. He grew in great demand as a poetry reader at pioneer gatherings and other celebrations.

Ultimately his hand grew unsteady, making it difficult for him to write. One of his last poems read:

If I had had along the grade
More light my steps attending
Less crooks I doubtless would have made,
less balks that needed mending.
And yet along the many years
My recollection traces
I've surely seen more smiles than tears,
More green, than desert places.

The farmer poet died in 1906 and was laid to rest in Evergreen Cemetery south of Cooper on Douglas Avenue, the route of the old plank road that Stoddard also immortalized in verse.

The Glory Days
of Grayling Fishing

The long narrow punt glided smoothly along the cold crystal clear waters of the Au Sable River. Ancient white cedars lined the banks and behind reared a dense forest of oak, beech, sycamore, maple and towering white pine. Each bend in the river brought new vistas, deer lapping the water, a high sandy rollway, huge dead cedars known as "sweepers," that had decades before toppled into the stream and now clawed out with jagged branches that made running the river an obstacle course. Nature's silence was broken only by the murmur of the river, the splash and gurgle of a great moss covered log that rose and sank leviathan like in the current, the drip of water off the long pole that propelled the craft and the plaintive groan of two tree branches rubbing together as they swayed in the breeze.

It was an August day in 1874. Thaddeus Norris, a sportsman who had traveled from Philadelphia for his first "raid" upon northern Michigan fish sat on the "live box" in the center of the boat, 12 foot rod in hand. As the craft swung around a bend Norris spotted a promising rift close by the overhanging bank. He spoke softly a few words to his "pusher," Len Jewel, who quietly laid the pole alongside and grabbing hold of some cedar branches brought the boat to a stop.

Norris deftly flicked his line, armed with three flies hand-tied with Guinea fowl, peacock and scarlet ibis feathers. The flies barely touched the surface of the stream when a fish struck, then another and another! They were small but spirited fighters, running upstream and leaping completely out of the water until exhausted they suddenly gave up to be pulled into the boat.

Norris unhooked his catch, slipped them through a hole in the side of the live box, through which river water circulated, and made another cast. The performance was repeated again and again. After making five casts Norris had taken 15 fish. The beautiful little fighters only weighed 6 to 18 ounces, but in that one day alone Norris and a companion from Bay City "killed and salted down - heads and tails off - a hundred and twenty pounds of fish, besides eating all we wanted."

Welcome to the glory days of Michigan fishing! And what kind of fish were they - so eager to take the hook and fight? The grayling - the greatest and most beautiful game fish to ever swim the peninsula's pure waters - a fish that lured sportsmen from around the world. Perhaps Saginaw sportsman William B. Mershon said it best:

Doubtless God could make a better fish than the Michigan grayling, but doubtless he never did. There are fishes of more brilliant coloring, but none surpass the peacock of its great dorsal fin and the rose pink of its caudal fin. None have a more graceful shape with lines trim and adapted to glide through the water with great ease.

Many were the contemporary witnesses who echoed Mershon's sentiments. Ansell Judd Northrup, a Syracuse, New York, lawyer, traveled to northern Michigan in 1879 for a week of grayling fishing on the Au Sable and Manistee rivers. He wrote:

The appearance of the grayling in the water, when hooked and excited and struggling, is something beautiful to see, - the large dorsal fin being the most conspicuous and noticeable feature. The colors of both the dorsal and pectoral fins are rich and delicate beyond description - the violet, pearly and golden tints and rainbow hues, marvelously contrasted and blended. The back is dark olive-brown; the sides and belly, silvery; the body, slim

The glorious grayling lured fishermen to Northern Michigan.

and graceful; the head small, mouth of medium size and tender; tail forked and broad; and the adipose fin shows his royal heritage

As if in keeping with their colorful appearance grayling would make a gaudy splash in the annals of 19th century Michigan and then disappear forever.

The European grayling which flourished in certain cold clear streams in England, France, Switzerland, Scandinavia and elsewhere was highly prized by early fishing authors. Isaac Walton wrote that the French valued the grayling so highly that "they say he feeds on gold, and that many have been taken out of their River of Loyre, out of whose bellies grains of gold have been taken."

A species of Arctic grayling was discovered in North America in 1819 by Capt. John Franklin's expedition toward the North Pole. The fish were not known to exist in American waters, however, until the mid 1850s when reports of a "new and peculiar kind of brook trout being caught in certain tributaries of the Muskegon River, and other northern streams of the state" reached Grand Rapids. The species was first dubbed "banner trout" in honor of its magnificent dorsal fin thought to resemble the American flag.

White on a business trip to the north in June, 1861, John T. Elliott of Grand Rapids, hired some Indians to catch banner trout in a small creek near Big Rapids. He preserved some in brine, giving samples to a Grand Rapids doctor who forwarded a specimen to Harvard professor Jean Louis Agassiz. The naturalist identified the fish as a new species of grayling - *Thymallus* (because when first taken from the water the fish smell like the herb thyme, although some say more like cucumber) *tricolor*. Notice of the fish appeared in a scientific journal in 1865 but did not attract the attention of many sportsmen until the early 1870s with the publication of a letter by Agassiz in newspapers across the country and discussions of the new fish in the popular journal *Forest and Stream*.

Dr. Daniel H. Fitzhugh, a Bay City real estate speculator, earned the title "father of the Grayling" through his promotion of and attempts to preserve the Au Sable grayling beginning in 1871. Fitzhugh took James W. Milner fishing there and following a spectacular outing in 1873 Milner published a series of popular articles about Michigan grayling.

Shortly thereafter according to Reuben Babbitt, a famous Au Sable fishing guide, upon learning that the species had been recognized as a sport fish much prized in Europe, the citizens of the Crawford County community founded as Crawford in 1872 held a mass meeting in the local railroad depot and promptly changed the site's name to Grayling. Those Grayling pioneers would not have been the first to recognize the commercial value to a name. Although it took the Jackson, Lansing and Saginaw Division of the Michigan Central which reached the site around 1873 a few more years to catch on. It first called its station Crawford while the post office had become Grayling by 1875. Within four years of that, however, both the post office and the railroad station adopted the name of the fighting fish as more and sportsmen took the train north to disembark at Grayling, the Au Sable River fishing headquarters.

Other railroads serving the north country also began capitalizing on the lure of the grayling. By 1875, the Grand Rapids and Indiana Railroad, "The Fishing Line," had begun promoting grayling fishing in the travel guides it distributed. By 1881, one such guide included an extensive account of the grayling and the testimonial of Col. George F. Akers, a Tennessee Fish Commissioner who had vacationed in northern Michigan:

I have caught the gamiest of all game fish, the American grayling. It is truly a daisy, pretty as a

Sweepers" on the Au Sable River made boating an adventure.

girl of sixteen, but harder to catch, and as superior to the speckled trout as the trout to the bass. Royal indeed, pure as the water it lives is, quick as thought in action, game to the last, the pride of the angler, and a sweet morsel for the hungry man when the offices of the cook are done and it is placed before you broiling hot."

What angler could resist such a recommendation? And come they did by the trainloads. One party of five from Detroit kept a record of their catch during a six day jaunt on the Au Sable in 1879. They hooked and kept a total of 950 grayling. They were not too particular about throwing back little ones, either, since the average weight of their catch was merely one third of a pound. Not until 1881 would Michigan establish a six-inch size limit on grayling. Fishing laws then, however, were little enforced, including legislation passed in 1875 that prohibited commercial sale of grayling. The fish were shipped out of state by the train carloads.

Babbitt included in his reminiscences that "from 1875 to 1888 father and I shipped our catches to a Chicago restaurant, which paid us the unheard of price of 25 cents a pound." Other sport and commercial fishermen alike greedily hounded the grayling. They filled their live boxes to overcapacity, the entire catch of 60 to 100 pounds would die and they would throw them away. Witnesses recorded "tons of grayling buried along the river and the banks of the Au Sable, Manistee and Jordan littered for miles with rotting grayling carcasses."

A few, like Northrup, saw the handwriting on the wall early on. He wrote in 1880:

He is a simple, unsophisticated fish, not witty, but shy and timorous. He is a "free biter," and is bound to disappear before the multitude of rods waved over his devoted head. The sport he affords in his capture, the taste he gratifies in the frying pan, and the allurements of the charming streams he inhabits, all conspire with his simplicity to destroy him. Could he but learn wisdom from his crimson - spotted cousin, and would the sportsman have pity on this beautiful and gentle creature of the smoothly gliding rivers, he would long live to wave the banner of beauty and glory in the cold, clear streams of the north. But that cannot be.

As if fishermen's greed were not enough, other factors conspired to eradicate the grayling. The logs of massive river drives conducted during the spawning time in the spring gouged the eggs out of the gravel and crushed the fry. Vast quantities of sawdust dumped in the streams by sawmills smothered the spawning grounds. Trout introduced into the grayling streams preyed on them.

Despite numerous attempts at artificial propagation and planting of grayling, the fish had disappeared from the Lower Peninsula by the turn-of-the-century. A few continued to exist in some Upper Peninsula streams such as the Otter River into the 1930s. Optimistic plans to transplant Montana grayling, a related species, to the Keweenaw Peninsula in the early 1960s proved largely a failure. Walton said St. Ambrose called the beautiful little creature "flower of fishes." That "flower" once native to Michigan blooms now only on the map.

Judge Flavius Littlejohn & His Indian Legends

Gray Wolf leaped beside the beautiful Indian princess, Mishawaha, who had spurned his affections for those of a white hunter named Dead Eye. "Through grating teeth and foam fletched lips, he hissed out the words, 'Vile slave of a pale-face dog; now die with him'."

He thrust his knife into her breast and she fell to the ground, murmuring: "I have saved his life, at the price of my own. He will avenge me. I die content." Within minutes Dead Eye had indeed accomplished his revenge, clubbing with his rifle butt the evil brave whose head "was crushed and flattened into a shapeless mass."

Ah, but the battle fought in 1801 between Leopold Pokagon's Potawatomi and Chief Elkhart's invading Shawnee warriors at the future site of Three Rivers was not over, not by any means. Would Dead Eye survive the conflict? Was lovely Mishawaha really dead? What role would the Potawatomi dwarf, Lynx Eye, play in this melodrama, par excellence?

To find the answer to those questions and more, you will need to turn to Flavius J. Littlejohn's *Legends of Michigan and the Old North West*, a 566 page volume published in Allegan in 1875. Based on oral histories collected from the very lips of the Indians and pioneers, many of the stories are set in the Kalamazoo River Valley. Although Littlejohn souped up the plot here and there and embellished some of the details, the book is regarded as "an interesting and authoritative account."

This classic volume was among the accomplishments of one of western Michigan's most illustrative pioneers. "Tall and commanding" with "dark piercing eyes," Littlejohn was a jurist,

Flavius Littlejohn's book of Indian legends contains numerous illustrations such as this battle scene.

geologist, surveyor, engineer, and legislator. He also came within a few thousand votes of being elected Michigan governor in 1849.

Born on July 20, 1804, in Litchfield, New York, Littlejohn's ancestry was Scotch and English. Following a typical frontier youth, he enrolled in Hamilton College in Clinton, New York, at the age of 20. Three years later he graduated as class valedictorian.

As was customary, he "read law" under an established attorney for three more years, then hung out his own lawyer's shingle. He soon won local fame for his legal skill. Unfortunately, so vigorously did he argue his cases that during one of his suites "he was taken with bleeding at the lungs in the court room."

Abandoning his chosen profession to regain his health, he immigrated to the newly established settlement of Allegan in the spring of 1836. There he first worked as a geologist and engineer. A jack-of-all-trades, he also resurveyed the original plat of the village, which had been found to be considerably less than accurate. In 1838, amid grandiose plans by the state legislature to dig a canal across the state to connect the Clinton and Kalamazoo Rivers, he surveyed the western end of the ill-fated scheme.

In 1841, Littlejohn launched his political career. He won election to the state legislature in 1842, 1845, and 1855. He also served as a state senator in 1845-46. Between legislative sessions, Littlejohn resumed his law career in Allegan.

Although he was ardently opposed to slavery, Littlejohn also believed in states rights - that the federal government had no right to universally abolish the "peculiar institution," and each state must decide for itself. In 1849, he ran as the gubernatorial candidate of the Free-Soil Party whose platform did not oppose slavery in the south only its extension into the new western territories. He was narrowly defeated by Democratic candidate John S. Barry of Constantine.

Eventually, Littlejohn found the principles of the Democratic Party more to his liking. In a state where the Republican Party had been founded in 1854, that proved unfortunate for his political career. Although he was well liked and respected his ambivalence on the abolition of slavery placed him in a minority position. During the Civil War he frequently delivered patriotic orations defending the Union and then rambled off into an "ill timed exposition of states rights," the very doctrine which had brought about succession by the southern states. E.C. Reid, editor of the Allegan *Journal*, recorded that at such times his fellow speakers on the platform had to get him back on the track via "vigorous pulls of his coat tails."

Littlejohn's forte, however, proved to be law. In 1858, he was elected circuit judge of a district that extended from Allegan County all the way to Grand Traverse, He made many hazardous trips with a swarm of lawyers in tow, dispensing justice at pioneer courtrooms scattered through the wilderness. L.G. Rutherford, an Oceana County attorney and Civil War veteran, recalled in 1882 some of what Littlejohn endured during the performance of his horseback circuit duties:

It would be hard to imagine, even, now, the hardships and inconvenience of journeys such as they performed; often losing their way by being unable to find the dim trail, they would be compelled to do what soldiers are sometimes allowed to do,"make themselves as comfortable as circumstances would allow, for the night."

In the process of making his way to frontier settlements he frequently stopped at Indian encampments and as a hobby Littlejohn collected

157

many of the legends and lodge stories retold in his 1875 volume.

Littlejohn, who had earned the nickname "old Trailer" as a result of his frontier wanderings, dedicated his "cluster of unpublished waifs, gleamed along the the uncertain, misty line, dividing traditional from historic times" to Henry Rowe Schoolcraft, the pioneer Michigan ethnologist in whose tracks he followed. While many of Littlejohn's stories are set in southern Michigan he also ventured into Schoolcraft's collecting area, the north country, to record legends of the Chippewa as well as the Ottawa Potawatomi, Sauk and Fox.

Judge Littlejohn died in 1880. Dignitaries and fellow lawyers arrived in Allegan in special black draped excursion trains and from 1,500 to 2,000 mourners solemnly marched to the tune of a brass band to the funeral ceremonies at Allegan's Oakwood Cemetery.

Originals of Littlejohn's 1875 volume have become scarce collector's items. Fortunately in 1956, the Allegan County Historical Society reprinted his book of Indian legends making it available for those who want to find out what happened to Mishawaha, Dead Eye and Lynx Eye.

Charles Blakeman,
Shanty Boy & River Hog

Red in the face, with rivulets of sweat coursing down their grimey cheeks and spattering on the dry forest floor, the "Charley team" glided a gleaming crosscut saw back and forth across the trunk of an ancient white pine. It was the early fall of 1879 in the woods near Cadillac. The Charley team, made up of Charley Brown from Traverse City and 17-year-old Charles Blakeman from Watson Township, Allegan County, had been well paired as to height and length of arms by the experienced eye of Dick Chilson, "bull" of the Copley & Lilly logging crew.

Despite their skill and experience in pulling together, the Charley team had met their match in that particular pine. The life blood of the forest giant, pitch, ran freely in the warm weather, clogging the teeth and causing the saw to pull hard. Periodically the men yanked the blade out of the kerf and doused it down from a flask of kerosene that dissolved the pitch. As they neared the heart of the pine they paused to pound in wedges that would prevent the trunk from settling back and crimping the saw.

The major problem, however, lay in the fact that an axe man had previously cut a notch in the trunk in the direction it was to fall - in this case straight across a wind fallen tree that stood a good chance of breaking the log when it fell.

Cookee had already blown his big tin gabriel signifying quitting time and making a bee line for the cook house the other shanty boys and teams of skidding oxen rushed past the sweating sawyers. But still the Charley team struggled on - the lumberjack's code forbade leaving a partly cut tree in the woods.

Big Chilson walked up to see what was the cause of the delay, and as the men sawed on, he began

159

driving the wedges in deeper. He scowled when he saw that the tree would land on the dead fall, but he kept quiet, realizing this would be a poor time to criticize the bone tired and hungry sawyers.

Suddenly came a sharp crack, a warning that the big pine would soon topple. The men stopped sawing and laid their faces along each side of the trunk, sighting the direction of the fall. Brown yelled "Your corner," and Blakeman answered "My corner."

The two deftly slid the saw around and rapidly zipped through the edge of the remaining wood on Blakeman's side causing the wood on the opposite corner to draw the tree in that direction. Blakeman yelled "Timberrr!" The huge pine began to slowly topple, picking up momentum, until with a ground shaking tremor it crashed, not onto the deadfall, but against a nearby maple tree. The enormous force of the collision uprooted the maple, but as the men had skillfully planned, it cushioned the fall and the big pine lay unbroken.

Chilson slapped his men on the back in congratulation of their feat and the three hastened to the cookhouse where they were soon wolfing down great helpings of salt pork, potatoes, baked beans and bread, in absolute silence as the law of the lumber camps decreed. About eight o'clock that evening, while the shanty boys sat around the "deacon's bench" in the bunk house swapping tall tales, Chilson arrived with a tally sheet in hand. "How many?" He called to each of the men, then noted down the number of trees they had felled that day. When the Charley team's time came, they both proudly yelled out "40," not a bad day's work with a cross cut saw.

Born in 1862 on the family's 40 acre farmstead located on the southern edge of Watson Township, three miles north of Otsego, Charles Elisher Blakeman had received his middle name in honor of an older

160

Typical northern Michigan shanty boys of Blakeman's era pose grudgingly for the camera.

brother, Elisher, who was killed in the Civil War. A few months later, his father also died, leaving the sole support of the five remaining children to his widow.

By the time he was 12-years-old Blakeman had begun supplementing the family's meager income through the operation of a trapline. During the summer, when fur was not valuable, he worked for area farmers at the rate of two bits a day and his meals. Because he needed to run his far ranging trapline in the colder months, Blakeman rarely attended the nearby Swan School. He later regretted his lack of education when he lost out on easier and better paying jobs in the lumber camps because he could not work with numbers.

In the fall of 1878, the husky 16-year-old set out for the northern lumber camps, where he secured a job near Stanton at the rate of $16.00 a month. The following season he went to Cadillac. That spring he pulled on caulked boots, swapped his axe and crosscut saw for a peavey and joined the dangerous life of the river hog. He rode the logs downstream to the mill, retrieving beached logs and breaking up log jams along the way. He also kept one eye peeled for signs of timber pirates who cut off the ends of logs branded with owner's initials and pounded on their own. When the river drive ended, he worked as a "frog," booming logs at a sawmill pond near Traverse City.

Eventually Blakemen left the Michigan piney woods for the Great West. He labored in Dakota Territory, building the Chicago, Milwaukee and St. Paul Railroad, logged at Rosebud in the Yellowstone River Valley and built roads across the California deserts.

By the 1920s age and a series of accidents had rendered him unfit for the strenuous life on the frontier. He set himself up in the business of printing greeting cards. Returning to Michigan he first opened a store in Kalamazoo, then moved to Grand Rapids where he settled down for good.

In 1928 Blakeman published a thin autobiographical volume, *Report of a Truant*, a picturesque and realistic account of how an Allegan County youth fared in the northern lumber camps. And in that little book he sold for 50 cents he offered a bit of hard earned wisdom for youth who would follow in his adventurous steps. It was as he was laboring in the California desert laying track while contemplating the luring power of a mirage he was seeing that the comparison come to him:

As these mirages lure from the trail, so did those lakes and woods of Michigan lure me from the way to get a better education, so now I'm sweating here in the desert to make money for those fellows that are at Long Beach and Santa Monica leaning back in easy chairs. Of course, I'm getting what I deserve, same as they are.

The Allegan
"Man-Eater"

With a thunder of hooves, the "Allegan man-eater" charged into the ring. The crowd of horse fanciers packed under the big top that winter's day in 1879 recoiled in involuntary horror. Despite the gelding's well earned reputation as "the most dangerous and vicious horse in the state, if not in the country" they were little prepared for what happened next. With bloodshot eyes gleaming like balls of fire, the horse reared and sprang ferociously at his trainer, biting, striking with his forelegs, kicking wildly. Breaking loose from the ropes and stakes that held him, he attacked the center pole, biting off great chunks of wood. Springing upon the bleachers he lunged desperately at anyone who met his eye, "screaming with rage when foiled in his attempt to seize his intended victim." As awesome as were his antics the spectators' exit from the tent proved nearly as dramatic. Several in their haste ripped holes in the canvas roof and jumped through to safety.

It was then, practically alone in the tent with the malevolent mount who had previously killed one man, crippled several for life and severely injured many more, that Prof. Dennis Magner, horse tamer par excellence, faced one of the greatest challenges of his 20 year career. And he fully intended to bring that beast to "subjection" or one of them would die in the process.

Magner had emigrated from Ireland at the age of 14, settling in western New York where he learned the art of carriage building. During the nine years he pursued that craft, he frequently traded horses for his products, as was the custom. Some of those horses proved unruly, surly or, of mean temperament. He encountered balkers and lungers, biters and kickers,

164

colts that threw themselves over backward, horses afraid of the rattle of a wagon, the sound of a gun, of dogs, hogs and open umbrellas. He got stuck with steeds prone to runaway, with cribbers and with more than one wind-sucker.

Faced with the prospect of loosing money on those bad trades, he began experimenting with various training methods and ultimately developed his own distinct techniques. Financial necessity also forced him to tackle veterinary problems and he learned remedies for bog spavin and capped hock, for the strangles and glanders, for the heaves, nasal gleet and flatulent colic, for sallenders, mallenders and a host of other loathsome sounding ailments which if you don't know what they are you probably don't want to.

Armed with this hard learned wisdom it was but natural for Magner to begin sharing his secrets with the public - for a fee of course. He conceived the idea of demonstrating his training techniques before "classes" of a dozen to several hundred spectators willing to lay out $5.00 for the honor. Frequently he would highlight his performance with attempts at breaking a particularly headstrong or vicious local horse. HIs first attempt to do so, staged in a barn, nearly ended in disaster when a mean spirited mare rushed for him with savage ferocity, ears laid back and mouth open wide. Magner managed to dive eight feet down into a hay mow, much to the hilarity of the spectators who had wisely climbed the barn's timbers prior to the mare's release. Magner dusted himself off, climbed back into the ring and after ten minutes of his treatments had so dizzied and repeatedly thrown the mare that she was completely tamed.

As Magner gained fame for his exploits while traveling throughout the eastern and midwestern states he encountered several notorious "man-eaters." In 1869 at Buffalo he went up against a big bay brute that had trampled a man to death and recently bitten the hand almost entirely off his handler. In 20 minutes time Magner had the horse so docile that he thrust his own hand right into its mouth.

As a sideline to his lucrative demonstrations Magner wrote a little 64 page treatise on horse training in 1863. The volume he hawked at his appearances grew larger and more comprehensive over the years.

The tenth revised edition of 208 pages appeared in 1871. By that year Magner had begun venturing into Michigan. Following a demonstration in Jackson in May, 1871, the Michigan Horse Breeder's association had "no hesitation in saying his system is the best in the world."

January of 1879 found Magner opening an amphitheatre "for the training and subjugating of wild and vicious horses" in Kalamazoo. The Kalamazoo *Gazette* noted "the perfection to which the science of horse training has been brought by Prof. Magner." From there he set up shop in Plainwell where 150 leading citizens signed a testimonial as to his success. Then he moved on to Allegan for his encounter with the man-eater.

While Magner had been earning fame for his horse taming exploits the Allegan equine contender had been achieving infamy for his wicked career. Even as a colt he had been "wonderfully wild," kicking and striking at anyone who approached. When lassoed for castration at the age of three, he had broke loose and it took several men on horseback an entire day to capture him and complete the operation. The next morning he proved so completely unmanageable, and what man could blame him, that he was allowed to run wild in pasture for the following two years.

An Allegan County farmer named Nathan Austin made the mistake of buying him then. Austin,

The Allegan "Man-eater" killing an Otsego man.

who had faced Confederate sharpshooters in the Atlanta Campaign as a member of the 14th Michigan Infantry, found that experience tame compared to dealing with the vicious horse. After it seriously injured him he sold it to E. Higgins. Hitched to Higgins' wagon, the horse kicked himself loose and smashed the vehicle to kindling. Higgins kept him two weeks before selling him to Lewis Hadden, another Otsego Township farmer. When the horse nearly kicked one of Hadden's sons to death John Hogle got him next. Hogle, a Civil War veteran who survived the bloody battles of Thompson's Station, Tenn. and Resacca, Ga., proved no better a match for the man-eater.

Dr. A.B. Way, another Civil War veteran who had established a practice in Allegan in 1873, took a chance on the horse next. He had him about a month when the horse kicked him to the floor of the stables. The physician saved his life by rolling under a manger, remaining imprisoned there until neighbors heard his yells. Not so lucky was Way's brother, who while attempting to feed the beast was kicked to death. The infuriated horse then "literally mangled his body by striking and kicking it about the stall."

Theodore E. Updyke, a 20-year-old post office clerk who had recently returned from Iowa to Allegan, owned the demented beast when Magner tried his skill. During that intense encounter Magner subjected the Allegan man eater to every trick he knew. He got his foreleg in a sling and repeatedly threw the maddened animal to the ground. He stretched a line between his tail and head forcing him to turn around and around in fury until dizzy. And finally he utilized his "third method of subjugation," passing a rope through the horse's mouth around and around the pressure point behind the ear.

As the horse was considered worthless untamed, Magner used his techniques to their utmost limits even at the risk of killing the animal. At the end of three hours the Kalamazoo *Gazette* reported that "the fury of the beast gave way before the superior intellect and science of man, and the horse became perfectly docile, allowing himself to be handled with ease and safety." The following day Updyke proudly drove his completely manageable steed up and down Allegan's crooked streets.

What ultimately befell the Allegan man-eater remains an historical mystery. Updyke left Allegan after a year for adventures in New Mexico, Arizona and Kansas, presumably taking his mount with him. He returned to Allegan in 1889 where he carved out a notable career in real estate and insurance.

Not long after Magner's supreme test with the Allegan man eater, he found himself a physical wreck, worn out by his two decades of battling vicious horses. In 1882 he checked into the Battle Creek Sanitarium, a famous health spa operated by corn flake, granola and peanut butter inventor, Dr. John Harvey Kellogg. The San evidently did him some good and Magner made Battle Creek his home over the following two decades. There he continued to compile successively more massive horse training guides - most of which highlighted his amazing transformation of the Allegan man-eater.

The Battle of Manton

Fully five hundred strong, the motley mass, self dubbed the "First Volunteer Regiment, Cadillac Militia," seethed down Manton's Wall Street on April 5, 1882. Clad in sloppy felt hats, flannel shirts, overalls and red suspenders, the familiar uniform of lumberjacks and lumber mill workers, the mob followed the commands of Wexford County Sheriff Charles C. Dunham, County Clerk T.J. Thorp and other county officials. Fifty of its number carried new repeating rifles, the rest clubs, canthook handles, crowbars and at least one broom.

Having fanned the flames of a decade of pent up desire during the 12 mile ride from Cadillac on railroad flatcars by downing an entire barrel of whiskey and numerous other flasks of fiery liquor, the militia closed in on its objective. Batting aside any Mantonite foolish enough to get in its way, the "Cadillackers" stormed the courthouse, battering in the door and barricaded windows with axes. Seizing the three big safes they had come for, they hustled them back to the train and victoriously made their way back to Cadillac while being regaled by the Marks Comedy Company brass band that had joined the jollity.

Comedy band aside, folks in Manton, especially the two left seriously injured, saw little humor in the loss of their court records during the epic Battle of Manton - an event Manton *Tribune* editor Charles Cooper branded "a more disgraceful scene never occurred in Michigan."

Both Cadillac and Manton owed their existence to similar factors: the Grand Rapids and Indiana Railroad that snaked its way north from Grand Rapids in the late 1860s and 1870s - the Chicago Fire of 1871 that created an unprecedented demand for Michigan lumber - and the prime tracts of virgin white pine that stretched over much of Wexford County.

George Mitchell, a talented financier, lumberman and entrepreneur, platted out a town site adjacent the railroad line along the eastern edge of Clam Lake in 1871. He originally called his town Clam Lake - not until 1877 would it take the more euphonious and historic appellation of Cadillac. Utilizing a canal connecting Big and Little Clam lakes (now lakes Mitchell and Cadillac) to float lumber to his site, Mitchell built a saw mill and soon Clam Lake emerged as a rip-roaring lumber town with numerous retails establishments, including as many as 36 taverns, to meet the need of the lumberjacks engaged in harvesting the surrounding timber. Other saw mills were established there and despite a fire that destroyed much of the business district in 1873 the community grew lustily to emerge as Wexford County's major population center.

Three other entrepreneurs saw potential in a town site adjacent the railroad twelve miles to the north. In 1872 Ezra Harger, Wexford County treasurer, J.S. Walling, a Free Will Baptist preacher, and George Manton, Colfax Township supervisor, founded the town they named after the supervisor. Harger put up a general store in the new town that first fall. The following season several sawmills went into production. The railroad built a depot, a blacksmith shop and hotel followed and within a year the community boasted 30 buildings and 150 residents.

In addition to burgeoning growth Manton and Cadillac had one other common factor - both sets of city fathers coveted the county seat status that had been awarded to a diminutive settlement to the east at a bridge over the Manistee River when Wexford County was created in 1869. The county seat,

171

originally called Manistee Bridge, then Sherman, lost whatever economic potential it had when the Grand Rapids and Indiana Railroad shifted the direction of its course away from Traverse City toward the Straits of Mackinac, thereby missing Sherman by about 15 miles.

Cadillac fired the first salvo of what would become a decade long Wexford County Seat War in October 1872 at the county supervisor's meeting. Cadillac supporters introduced a resolution to hold a public election on the question of moving the county seat from Sherman to their community. It required a two thirds majority to pass such a resolution and the supervisors voted it down handily five to four. If the county's electorate were to vote on the proposition it would require only a simple majority and Cadillac's larger population could achieve that easily. But without the support of two thirds of the supervisors that election could never be held.

As the war raged throughout the 1870s Cadillac and Manton advocates attempted various schemes. New townships were creating to add supervisors. Cleon Township was detached from Manistee County and attached to Wexford County. Cadillac adopted a city charter which gave it three additional votes, and bribes were allegedly offered to supervisors to change their vote. Sherman, seeing the handwriting on the wall, began backing Manton's efforts. Still the two thirds majority eluded either side.

Then Cadillac supporters conceived a devious stratagem. They began privately cajoling members of the Manton block, telling them that since Cadillac's case looked hopeless, Manton would be the next best site. They promised to back Manton against Sherman - but if anything went amiss then Manton should support Cadillac. Little did the Mantonites know but Cadillac was making similar overtures to other aspirants for the county seat such as Meauwataka, sited at the geographic center of the county. By 1878, the ruse seemed to have worked and the supervisors passed a resolution to put the matter of the move from Sherman to Manton to the voters. Unfortunately the electorate had not been sufficiently informed of their role in the scheme and Sherman and Cadillac citizen voted an emphatic no.

They tried again in the April 1881 election and this time the Cadillac voters had been amply briefed - the move to Manton passed 1,109 to 146. Mantonites lit huge bonfires and celebrated to the wee hours. Their exhilaration would be short lived.

Manton had pledged to construct a courthouse, which it did, but the sheriff, county clerk, and treasurer soon found the building inadequate and conducted business elsewhere. Widely distributed handbills accused Manton of failing to build a decent courthouse and Cadillac merchants and mill owners promised to erect a suitable palatial structure at no expense to the county. Cadillac supporters failed by only one vote in getting their city designated the site of a new county jail.

The Cadillac controlled board of supervisors soundly defeated any appropriation for Manton's county seat related expenses. Then Sheriff Dunham and County Clerk Thorp designated Cadillac the official site for holding circuit court.

The June 14, 1881, supervisors' meeting was held in two places - Manton supporters met in Manton and the Cadillac block held a rump session in Cadillac. Both sides declared the other's meeting illegal. In August supervisors at a Cadillac session voted to carve Harding Township, adjacent the city, into six miniature townships. Elections were held and new supervisors loyal to the Cadillac cause voted in. Manton felt secure that it could block this move as illegal. But it never got the chance.

At a special supervisor's meeting held on

The soldiers of the Battle of Manton included the likes of these local mill workers.

February 14, 1882, the seating of the new supervisors was referred to committee, and they were never seated. Their votes proved unnecessary because at that meeting George Blue, previously a loyal Manton supporter, suddenly swung his vote in favor of Cadillac. Bribery charges leveled at Blue by Manton backers were never positively proved. Nevertheless Cadillac had secured the necessary two thirds vote and an election to decide whether to move the county seat to that city was promptly set for April 4th.

The vote went pretty much as expected - 1,363 for removal to Cadillac and 309 against. But two northern townships loyal to Manton had destroyed their ballots and refused to make a return - thus raising the grounds for legal action. Manton advocates might well seek an injunction prohibiting the removal of county records prior to the official canvas of the election. Cadillac strategists planned to counter that threat by quickly moving the records before an injunction could be issued - *fait accompli!*

The political jockeying was over - now it was time to get physical. Accordingly, early in the morning following the election a train consisting only of a locomotive, tender, caboose, one boxcar and one flatcar rolled to a stop about 100 feet from the Manton Courthouse. Sheriff Dunham and a contingent of special deputies climbed down to be met by County Clerk Thorp who unlocked the courthouse. Within 30 minutes they had lugged most of the county records and furniture aboard the train.

They were in the process of moving the safe in the treasurer's office when Manton reacted. According to the Manton version of the story ten or twelve citizens confronted 60 deputies and politely asked Dunham by what authority he was acting. The drunken sheriff arrogantly replied "he did not have to have any authority!" Whereupon the Manton men overturned the safe, one of deputies drew a handgun,

175

a fight broke out and the "Cadillackers" were driven back to the train and out of town.

The Cadillac version had a mob of 200 Manton bullies attack a mere 20 deputies who retreated in order to protect the records already aboard the train.

The two versions of what happened next during the second Battle of Manton bear even less similarity, and it is unlikely the exact scenario will ever come to light. Suffice it to say that about noon a second train reached Manton, loaded with anywhere from 300 to 600 Cadillac officials, mill hands, a visiting brass band, and other citizens, armed with rifles, clubs, etc. Most had imbibed liquor to a greater or lesser extent. They faced either an angry mob of Mantonites plus every able bodied farmer for miles around or merely 60 peaceable citizens. At least two Manton supporters were injured, the door to the courthouse battered down and the safes carried away. Intrigueing but apocryphal variants range from a contingent of Manton women greasing the rails with butter and lard to prevent the train from leaving, and the secret burial of a Manton casualty with an axe still embedded in his corpse, to squads of drunken 12-year-old Cadillac hooligans beating citizens unmercifully.

Whatever actually happened on April 5, 1882, the two Battles of Manton had definitely decided the outcome of the ten year Wexford Courthouse War in Cadillac's favor. Despite the negative publicity that flooded state newspapers concerning Cadillac's heavy handed action the county seat stayed there - although a courthouse would not be erected until 1911 - at taxpayers expense.

Today if you visit Manton, decorated with leprechauns and four leaf clovers in honor of the annual Irish festival began in 1976, you can read a general version of the Battle of Manton on an official Michigan historical marker erected adjacent the Manton Museum.

And if you happen to talk to one of the community's older residents, say seated within the Shamrock Tavern, located, incidently, at the site of the short-lived Manton Courthouse, you might hear one other interesting version of that fateful battle of 1882. It seems an Irishman named Cousins was sitting outside Benson's Saloon, probably waiting for it to open, when the first Cadillac invasion approached. He promptly tried to stop the deputies with his fists. And as his friends testified many times, had there been two more Irishmen to assist nothing would have left the courthouse that morning. Having known more than a few Irishmen, who knows, maybe they were right.

George E. Bardeen, Otsego Paper Monarch

Otsego, "would be little more than a four corners" were it for not the influence of George E. Bardeen, noted the Otsego *Union* at the time of his death on January 26, 1924. Eulogistic hyperbole aside, there was a good deal of truth to that statement. "Internationally known as the dean of the paper manufacturing industry of Michigan,"Bardeen brought to his hometown the two paper mills that continue to provide a major element in that Allegan County community's economy.

Born November 10, 1850, in Fitchburg, Mass., when he was eight-years-old Bardeen lost his father. Two years later, his mother remarried an up-and-coming young shopkeeper named Samuel A. Gibson. In 1865, the Gibsons moved to Kalamazoo, leaving Bardeen to finish his education at the Randolph Normal School in Vermont and a business college at New Haven, Connecticut.

In the meantime, in concert with Benjamin F. Lyon, Gibson launched the pioneer paper mill of the Kalamazoo Valley in 1867. At a water powered mill located south of Kalamazoo on Portage Creek, the Kalamazoo Paper Company first manufactured a rough grade of paper made from bleached straw. A few years later, it expanded into production of finer paper.

In 1868, Bardeen joined his stepfather's fledgling business as a bookkeeper. Over the succeeding two decades he advanced to the position of secretary of the company. During that period a majority of the men who would establish the paper mills that dotted the Kalamazoo River Valley in the early 20th century received their training at the Kalamazoo Paper Company under Gibson's guidance.

Bardeen set the example for his fellow employees to follow in 1887 when he resigned from the Kalamazoo Paper Company and organized the Bardeen Paper Company. Of several communities on the Kalamazoo River under consideration, Bardeen choose Otsego primarily because of a fortunate circumstance for the languishing village. Due to a recent flood it offered the only available site not under water at the time. Situated between the Kalamazoo River mill race and the Michigan Southern Railroad tracks, the original Bardeen mill was at the site of the current Menasha Paper Company. The rail line provided excellent transportation facilities and the Kalamazoo River offered a source for the huge quantities of water required in papermaking as well as an efficient means of disposing of the waste products.

Otsego recognized the importance the new paper mill would have in reviving its dormant ecomony. The laying of the corerstone of the mill in May, 1887, brought a general holiday for the village. Prominent orators made speeches, the Otsego Military Band played lively airs and local school children sang lyrics penned for the occasion by James M. Ballou:

"We welcome you from Kal 'mazoo,
We meet you with good will;
We greet you and your hammer's sound,
That builds the Bardeen Mill."

The structure stood complete in October and the big paper machine spewed out its first product two months later. Bardeen's business boomed. In 1892, a second mill, situated off the west side of Farmer Street near the south bank of the Kalamazoo River went into operation. By 1903 the Bardeen Paper Company had become the largest manufacturing plant in Allegan County, capable of producing over 300 tons of paper weekly. Four

Bardeen No. 1 Mill, Otsego, Mich.

In 1911 Bardeen's No. 1 Mill stretched along the Kalamazoo River in Otsego.

hundred and fifty employees worked at its four mills in Otsego. Women comprised forty percent of Bardeen's labor force, earning a wage of $5.00 to $11.00 per 60 hour work week, based on a piece rate.

Bardeen erected an opulent "Queen Anne" style mansion on Allegan Street complete with a ball room and bowling alley and heated by steam pipes which ran from one of his paper mills. Torn down in the 1960s, the site is currently occupied by a laundromat.

Active in civic affairs, Bardeen served as village president and he headed up the Otsego Board of Education. Known by fellow Otsegoites as an affable man "of a genial social nature," he boosted the school band and athletic program and personally financed a city baseball team. For his employees he established reading rooms, gymnasiums, a kindergarten and other progressive programs.

In 1903 Bardeen and Fred Lee of Dowagiac established the Lee Paper Company in Vicksburg. Two years later, Bardeen took a leading role in the creation of another large paper mill in Otsego named MacSimBar, an amalgam of Bardeen's name and those of the other founders, his son-in-law M.B. McClellan and General Superintendent of the Bardeen Mills W.S. Simpson.

In March, 1905, Bardeen called a special meeting at the Otsego Opera House to introduce the proposition to the citizens and offer them the opportuinity to buy stock in the new venture. Local investors soon put up $120,000 of the $150,000 needed. By September 70 men using horse drawn scrapers had begun work on the mill site, a swampy area in the northwest section of Otsego, north of the river. Spcial white bricks arrived from the renowned Veneklasen brick yards in Zeeland.

On August 23, 1906, the first paper came off the huge foundrinier machine and by 1909 with the construction of a 180 feet high steel smoke stack MacSimBar was producing 250 tons of paper each week. The mill ultimately became one of the country's leading producers of paper board. The MacSimBar Mill currently operates under the name, Rock-Ten Company.

In addition to his leadership in paper making Bardeen served as president of the Citizens State Savings Bank of Otsego, the Kalamazoo Stove Company and the Globe Casket Company of Kalamazoo.

In 1922, the Bardeen Paper Company merged with the Monarch Paper Company and the King Paper Company to form the Allied Paper Mills. Bardeen served as a director of that new corporation until his death during a Florida vacation in 1924.

A biographical piece published in 1927 noted "in his death the state and nation lost a loyal citizen who had given the best years of his life toward the upbuilding of the better interests of his adopted state and home community."

Classic Ceramic Souvenirs
Capture
Mackinac Memories

Something there is about human nature that craves momentoes - souvenirs of visits to exotic places, mnemonic devices that summon up memories of happy times, gifts for loved ones who could not come, or packrat acquisitions to swell "curiosity cabinets."

The pioneer tourists who fell under the lure of Mackinac Island in the 1830s and 1840s carried home agate pebbles plucked up where Lake Huron laps the "big turtle," miniature mococks of maple sugar - handmade Indian artifacts fashioned from buckskin, birch bark, black ash, porcupine quills and sweetgrass. A century and a half later the hordes that pour on and off the ferry boats each half hour lug away tee shirts and ball caps, rubber tomahawks made in Japan and cartons of fudge to buoy their memories. Now, baseball caps are fun and fudge is good but as souvenirs they don't have the lasting power that historians prefer.

But, in between the black ash baskets and the fudge came a gentler, kinder era, a turn-of-the-century time when tourists left the island with wicker suitcases and steamer trunks carefully packed with classic souvenirs, delicate hand painted china plates, bud vases, cups and saucers, salt shakers, toothpick holders, pill boxes and pipe rests emblazoned with detailed colorful views of the island's many attractions. Once considered mere knickknacks, geegaws and dust catchers, these fragile commemoratives have survived the vicissitudes of time in attic trunks, and curved glass china cabinets, in antique shops and flea markets and increasingly in collector's cases to continue to provide memories as well as historical sources decades after the tourists who bought them passed on.

Production of ceramic ware with views of American scenery and prominent buildings dates back to the 1820s. From 1820 to 1850 inexpensive earthenware pieces decorated with deep blue transfer views were produced by potters in Staffordshire, England, and imported in large quantities for the American market. These so called "Historical Blue China" pieces sold cheaply and were intended for everyday use.

But the concept of marketing pictorial china as souvenirs did not emerge until the late 1880s. That came about largely through the efforts of midwestern entrepreneur C.E. Wheelock. He began in Janesville, Wisconsin, in 1888 and six years later reestablished his flourishing business in South Bend, Indiana. By the turn-of-the-century he had opened a branch office in Peoria, Ill. Much of Wheelock's success lay behind his marketing techniques. He employed as many as 15 agents to travel the country canvasing gift shops and novelty stores in resorts like Mackinac Island, Sault Ste. Marie and Mt. Clemens as well as small out-of-the way villages.

Wheelock's agents pitched his varied line of china blanks ranging from tiny bud vases, toothpick holders, pill boxes, butter pats, larger plates, cups and saucers, mugs and reticulated oval bowls to porcelain novelties such as shoes, boots, top hats, buckets and watering cans. Merchants could select the views they wanted pictured in color on the pieces from existing post cards or other printed sources or a unique design would be rendered. As a final sales clincher the merchant's name could be stamped on the bottom of each piece.

Wheelock utilized a variety of porcelain factories in Germany and Austria, long noted for their quality output of "bone china," to manufacture the stock ordered. The view was printed on tissue paper and transferred to the china. Artists sometimes colored the views by hand or at least highlighted the details and added floral backgrounds and gilt borders. Despite the costs of hand coloring, importation and tariffs these quality ceramic souvenirs sold at prices cheap even at turn-of-the-century standards. In 1905 Wheelock advertised plates decorated with three to six colored views and gilt edges that "retailed at ten cents each, netting the dealer a good profit."

The McKinley Tariff Act of 1890 stipulated that wares imported into America be identified as to the country of origin and each Wheelock piece included that information, his name and often the customer's as well. Wheelock's salesmen met with success on Mackinac Island. Among the many pieces of Wheelock china extant are five and one half inch diameter plates featuring colored views of Arch Rock, Fort Mackinac and the Grand Hotel, made in Germany and imported by Wheelock for C.H. Parrott; a view of the fort's block house made for John S. Doud and the ever popular view of a sailboat framed by Arch Rock made and imported for J. H. Schwegler. The latter merchant appears in the Mackinac Island section of *Polk's Business Gazetteer of Michigan* for 1909 as one of the island's ten "curio" dealers.

That year, 1909, witnessed the creation of a souvenir china importing firm that would rival Wheelock's success. John H. Roth, who had worked for Wheelock earlier, also established his company in Peora, Illinois. The porcelain pieces he imported from Germany carry his logo on the reverse, the outline of an artist's palette and the words "Hand painted, Germany - The Jonroth Studios." Roth, also, identified his customers on the reverse. Typical of his work is a four inch tall creamer picturing Fort Mackinac imported for Jape's Art Shop on the island and a view

Full view Jonroth plates capture in ceramic Fort Mackinac and Arch Rock.

of the fort's block house overlooking the village imported for C.H. Wickman, who is listed as a "photo dealer" in the 1909 *Polk's Gazetteer.*

Jonroth hand painted plates with detailed images covering the entire front of the plate range from five to nine inches in diameter and are arguably the most spectacular of the entire field of souvenir china.

Competition from Roth and others put Wheelock out of the souvenir china business in the early 1920s. The Jonroth Company continued well into the 1970s, although importation of pottery from Germany and Austria ended with the outbreak of World War II. While Wheelock and Jonroth were the big names in souvenir china there were numerous other importers whose wares usually were merely marked as "Made in Germany" although some also identified such Mackinac Island customers as Stewart & Preston and K. Geha & Bros.

Among the china most coveted by collectors are pieces bearing a gleaming cobalt blue background. Cobalt souvenirs appear in a bewildering variety of sizes, shapes and images of island attractions including Old Mission Church, the Father Marquette Statue, Sugar Loaf and Arch Rock. More than 20 varient views of the latter natural wonder have survived on German-made souvenir china.

The Great Depression and the beginning of World War II coupled with competition from cheaper stock imported from Japan spelled the end of this golden era of pictorial souvenir china. In general, the vast majority of "Made in Germany" pictorial souvenir china dates from the first three decades of the 20th century.

Researching when merchants for whom the china was imported remained in business can more closely bracket the age of the individual pieces. Sometimes close examination of the view depicted and a bit of historical detective work can also yield more precise dating. For example, a piece picturing the Father Marquette Statue, erected in 1909, has to date from that year or later. A butter pat picturing the sidewheel steamer, the *City of Mackinac*, coursing through the waves, dates from the period 1893 when the vessel was launched to 1912 when it was renamed the *City of Mackinac II*. This fast 275 foot long Detroit and Cleveland Steam Navigation Company steamer carried hundreds of thousands of recreationists to Mackinac Island prior to its acquisition by the Goodrich Transit Company in 1922 which renamed it the *City of Holland*.

And while excursionists no longer steam up from Detroit on such palatial vessels as the *City of Mackinac* it is possible to return to that glorious era in Mackinac Island's past by savoring the same delicate porcelain pieces that those tourists of 70 to a 100 years ago carried home to help preserve memories of the island's incomparable beauty, charm and historic appeal.

Galesburg's Hometown Hero: Gen. William R. Shafter

Short tempered on the best of days, 63-year-old Major General William Rufus Shafter, a great walrus of a man who tipped the platform scales at 300 pounds, could "swear till the air'd pop and the breezes'd spit red fire." And that fateful morning of June 22, 1898, as the invading American army under his command sailed toward Daiquiri, Cuba, to launch a beach landing with potentially heavy resistance from entrenched Spanish defenders, was definitely not the best of days. As if the stifling heat and tenseness of the situation were not enough, Richard Harding Davis, an arrogant young war correspondent, had been persistently wheedling the general to change his orders and allow him a special berth in a landing craft. It was when Davis informed Shafter that he "was not an ordinary reporter but a descriptive writer" that he snapped, barking out "I do not give a damn what you are! I'll treat all of you alike!"

Shafter had wrestled to the ground many a bully in the Galesburg of his youth. He had faced with determination and courage Confederate minnie balls and bayonet charges. He had looked in the face of death in the form of Apache arrows and outlaw bushwackers on the Texas frontier. But all his dauntless courage and military acumen would come to naught when he dared to defy the power of the press.

Shafter's pioneer father, Hugh, had emigrated from Vermont to Michigan Territory in 1833. Selecting 200 acres in Section 13, of Kalamazoo County's Comstock Township, just north of Galesburg, he built a log cabin, plowed and planted 40 acres and returned to Vermont. He was back in time for harvest that fall of 1834 with his new young wife. On the 16th of October, 1835, she delivered a husky baby they named William Rufus. The monotonous cycle of work on the Galesburg farm proved little to young Shafter's liking. He preferred roaming the woods, hunting raccoons and bee trees, and he became a expert rifle marksman. He also earned a reputation as a wrestling champion, gaining the nickname "Bull" among fellow students in the local one-room school.

Following graduation from the eighth grade Shafter became a teacher himself. His fighting skills stood him in good stead in the classroom, the custom of the times being that a teacher needed to best the bully of the school to win the respect of the student body. S.A. Carleton, one of his childhood friends, later remembered how Shafter "would knock down and drag out his victims, as some times occurred at spelling schools or exhibitions when rough-necks would interrupt the exercises and some of them would go out of a window."

The spring of 1861 found Shafter attending the Richland Seminary, a type of private high school. The stirring events at Fort Sumpter and President Lincoln's call for volunteers to defend the Union inspired the 26-year-old school teacher to join the colors. On June 28th he was mustered in as a lieutenant in the 7th Michigan Infantry.

Shafter first saw action in the Battle of Ball's Bluff, Virginia, on October 21, 1861, a disastrous loss to the Union regiments commanded by Brig. Gen. Charles P. Stone. The 7th Michigan then participated in the bloody Peninsular Campaign and Shafter fought in the siege of Yorktown and the battles of West Point, Fair Oaks, Savage Station, Glendale and Malvern Hill.

Wounded during the Battle of Fair Oaks, Shafter remained on the field, furnishing "beautiful exhibitions of gallant conduct and intelligent activity." Three decades later he was belatedly awarded the Congressional Medal of Honor for his heroism during that battle.

Shafter's military leadership so impressed his commanders that he was promoted directly from lieutenant to major of the 19th Michigan Infantry on September 5, 1862. His unit faced its biggest challenge of the war on March 4th and 5th, 1863, during an engagement at Thompson's Station, Tenn. In company with Wisconsin, Ohio and Indiana regiments the 19th Michigan fought three tough Confederate brigades including Gen. Nathan Bedford Forrest's celebrated cavalry. That bloody battle witnessed fierce cavalry and bayonet charges on both sides and Shafter distinguished himself with his daring. But the 19th Michigan ultimately was forced to surrender. In respect for his bravery the Confederates permitted Shafter to retain his sidearms and horse after the capture. Nevertheless, he languished in notorious Libby Prison at Richmond, Va., for two months before being exchanged.

Returning to duty after his release, Shafter was promoted to lieutenant-colonel in June, 1863, and the following year he was appointed full colonel in command of the 17 U.S. Colored Infantry. Despite being equipped with inferior old weapons, Shafter whipped his black troops into such a high state of discipline and morale that during their first engagement before Nashville, Tenn., in December, 1864, "they fought regularly and vehemently, like regular soldiers."

A few months after the war ended at Appomattox Courthouse, Shafter was breveted Brig. General for his "gallant and meritorious services" during four years of combat.

Following the war came a drastic reduction of the military forces and Shafter was mustered out of the army. But the citizen soldier had developed a taste for army life and he campaigned for appointment in the regular army. Thanks to numerous recommendations including that of Maj. Gen. George H.. Thomas, Shafter won appointment as lieutenant-colonel of the 41st U.S. Infantry in January 1867. Two years later he was assigned as commander of another black regiment, the 24th Infantry.

Then came ten long years of campaigning with his "buffalo soldiers" on the isolated Texas frontier, engaged in intermittent Indian warfare and forays against border bandits. His troopers affectionately nicknamed him Pecos Bill and as one would-be poet later recalled:

"Don't hardly reckon there even was a tougher ol' soldier pill,

In any way that you'd size him up, than that same ol' Pecos Bill,"

Shafter became colonel of the 1st Infantry in 1879 and eight years later finally regained the rank of brig.-general, serving in the Department of Columbia and the Department of California.

The year 1898 brought a great personal loss with the death of his wife, the former Harriet Amelia Grimes of Athens, Michigan. But it also offered Shafter a chance of the lifetime opportunity to demonstrate to his nation the military leadership he had spent four decades in developing.

American popular attitudes toward Spanish tyranny in Cuba, Gen. "Butcher" Weyler and his concentration camps, had been whipped into a frenzy during the "gay 90's" by sensational "yellow press" journalism. In addition, the martial ambitions of a younger generation eager to prove itself in battle and the lure of territorial expansion offered underlying motives. The sinking of the battleship *Maine* on February 15, further enflamed the national mood and on April 25, 1898, Congress declared war on Spain with the objective to free Cuba.

The advent of war found the American Army in

En route to the Cuban front Gen. Shafter's mount earned new meaning to the term "beast of burden."

a deplorable state of readiness, ill equipped and under strength. With hurried preparations under way to raise volunteer regiments and cobble together the quantities of supplies and equipment required by an invasion force, President William McKinley called a White House conference to choose a commander for the American expeditionary force. Nelson A. Miles, Major General Commanding the Army, reportedly glanced at the list of candidates, then placing his finger on Shafter's name said: "If you want a man with force and ability to insure the success of such a task, there is the man to do it!" Secretary of War Russell A. Alger, also a Michigan man, promptly announced Shafter's selection.

As the growing army of recruits trained in southern camps, suffering from the heavy wool uniforms they were issued and substandard rations dubbed by the men "embalmed beef," the modern American "steel navy," which had been ready for war, "remembered the *Maine*." On May 1, Commodore George Dewey's Asiatic squadron annihilated the Spanish squadron at Manila Bay. The Spanish ships in the Caribbean ducked into Santiago Harbor to be bottled up by Admiral William Sampson's and Commodore Winfield Schley's fleet.

After over a month's delay while he awaited formal orders, Shafter launched his invasion force comprising 32 transports carrying nearly 16,000 troops from his headquarters in Tampa, Florida, on June 12. With objectives to reinforce Sampson and Schley and seize the port of Santiago, Shafter's force landed without resistance at Daiquiri and Seboney Bay to the east on June 22.

Despite the fact that he suffered from fever and gout much of the time and sometimes needed to be carted around on a door, the corpulent commander accomplished his mission. His soldiers fought their way to the heights east and north of Santigo, placing their artillery in position to shell the city and the Spanish fleet in the harbor.

When the Spanish fleet under Admiral Cervera tried to run the blockade on July 3, it was destroyed during a four hour engagement. The 24,000 troops garrison at Santigo surrendered to Shafter two weeks later and for all practical purposes the "splendid little war" was over.

Shafter had accomplished his mission with relatively little loss of American life - yet due largely to his encounter with Davis and the press corp off the coast of Daiquiri he received little but sarcasm, second guessing and blame from most journalists. One reporter admitted that following his order not permitting newspapermen on the initial landing "pencils began to be sharpened for Gen. Shafter." Those vindictive pencils would succeed in all but destroying the reputation earned during a long and faithful military career. Conversely, flamboyant Teddy Roosevelt and his "Rough Riders," the darlings of the press, earned a reputation far in excess of their actual role - and the cowboy soldier would be launched on his way to the White House.

Nevertheless, Michigan folks remained mighty proud of their home grown hero. After the war Shafter made a triumphant tour to the site of his early life. Kalamazoo staged a massive parade complete with the presentation of a prize head of celery "fresh as the dew from Kalamazoo," while a float of pretty "celery city queens" chanted "Who are we after... who are we after... We are after... General Shafter."

Shafter retired from the service in 1901, dying at his home near Bakersfield, California five years later. In 1919, Galesburg citizens remembered their hometown hero with the dedication of a bronze bust of Shafter sculpted by Pompeo Coppini of Chicago. There atop a granite base Shafter's likeness continues to proudly survey his boyhood haunts.

Todd's Big Barn

Visitors traveled from around the world to ogle at Albert M. Todd's big barn. Well they might. Built to accomodate 500 head of cattle, it was six times the size of what others thought a big barn. It was a barn fit for a king - a peppermint king, that is.

The huge structure was located on what is now known as 118th Avenue, northwest of the little creek that cuts across the "Todd Farm" wildlife refuge in Allegan County's Ganges Township. At the turn-of-the-century Todd's big barn was the focal point of the mint plantation and company town he had established there and proudly named "Campania."

Todd owned 1,640 acres at Campania, 2,000 acres at another mint farm in Van Buren County, named Mentha and a 7,000 acre cattle ranch called Sylvania in Newaygo County. Those holdings and the fact that his Kalamazoo based refinery processed close to 90% of the world's supply of peppermint oil well earned him the title "peppermint king."

Born on a small farm near Nottawa, St. Joseph County, in 1850, Todd was the youngest of ten children. Following graduation from Sturgis High School he studied chemistry briefly at Northwestern University. In 1868, Todd and an older brother, Oliver, first experimented with the growing and distillation of peppermint which had been grown commercially in a small way in St. Joseph County beginning in 1835. Todd used his training as a chemist to develop an improved method of rectifying the oil which resulted in a purer product.

By 1891, when he moved his headquarters to Kalamazoo, the A.M. Todd Company had established a reputation for quality that placed it in the forefront of the mint industry. In addition to his relentless pursuit of quality control and the development of tests and standards, he imported hardier, more productive varieties from England and advocated moving mint growing areas from the traditional prairie soils to muck lands.

Todd's first attempt to develop extensive muck acreage for the cultivation of mint in the Decatur area around 1892 was foiled because of the high cost of the land. By 1895 he had acquired his swampy Mentha and Campania holdings at a much cheaper rate.

Actually, an entrepreneur named Henry F. Severens had pioneered mint growing in Allegan County. By 1896 he had the "largest peppermint field in the world," fully a mile long, in operation in the area directly east of the Todd farm. The entire muck area south of Hutchin's Lake, in fact, was known as the Severens Marsh.

So wet was the soil at Campania, that 10 miles of canals and drainage ditches were required. Then horses equipped with special muck shoes, 12 inch wide iron plates invented by Decatur mint grower, Lyscom Brigham, pulled plows unearthing long furrows three feet apart. At the height of the growing season, Todd employed 100 men and an equal number of horses at Campania. The mint growing cycle involved planting the root stock by hand, hoeing weeds until July, mowing the plants, allowing them to cure like hay and piling that mint hay on wagons for transport to the distillery. There the mint oil was extracted by steam pressure.

Overproduction in the 1890s brought a glut on the market and the average price of mint oil dropped from $8.00 to .70 cents per pound. In order to make any profit at all growers began curing the mint hay after the oil had been removed and feeding it to livestock. About that time Todd got the idea for his mammoth barn.

Constructing a secure foundation for his huge

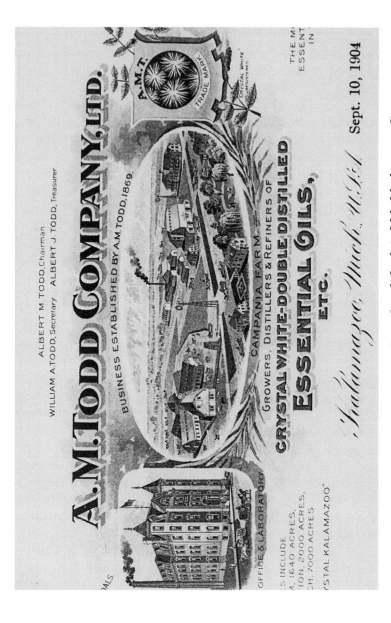

The Todd Company letterhead depicted his big barn at Campania.

building in the soft muck proved his first big challenge. He accomplished that by pouring 168 concrete piers on the "hardpan" below the muck. Pumps in constant operation kept the water out until the concrete hardened. One thousand loads of sand went into and around the foundation for the six, 26 feet diameter silos that stood at the center of the barn. From those silos six barns capable of storing 3,000 tons of hay and accommodating 500 cattle radiated out like the points of a star.

Todd's plan was simple but ingenious. His herd of cattle summered on the vast range he held in Newaygo County. In the fall they were rounded up and shipped by rail to nearby Pearl and driven to the big barn. Throughout the winter they were fattened up on mint hay and silage and sold in the spring. This process also solved another problem. Because mint cultivation rapidly depleted even rich muck soil, it was necessary to return the hay's nutrients to the land. The hay itself was difficult to plow under, until it had been run through the cattle, that is.

Unfortunately Todd's big star shaped barn burned down shortly after the turn-of-the-century. Nevertheless with the addition of another large storage barn the Campania operation continued strong.

By 1913, 17 structures dotted Campania, including a large family mansion, a tin shop which manufactured mint oil cans, a company store, a school house for employee's children, three mint stills and a row of worker's houses purchased pre-cut from a Sears Roebuck catalog. In addition to 1,000 acres of mint, Todd later diversified into vegetables, sugar beets and broom corn. During World War I he grew hemp for making rope.

In the meantime Todd carved out a notable career distinct from his mint empire. He excelled as a book and art collector and many of the fine pieces he brought back from Europe have survived in Kalamazoo museums and educational institutions. He became interested in various reform efforts including public ownership of utilities. Running as a Democrat in a district that had been solidly Republican since the party's birth in 1854, he became the only Democratic congressman elected from Michigan in 1896.

But the verticillium wilt disease that struck the Michigan mint district in the 1920s sounded the death knell for Campania and Mentha. The A.M. Todd Co. continued as the world's leading producer of mint oils but no longer was it grown locally. Todd died in 1931 and his family converted Campania into a wildlife sanctuary during the depression.

In 1950 the State of Michigan acquired Campania and much of the Severens holdings. Most of the buildings were torn down, although one three-story barn was disassembled and rebuilt at Hickory Corners where it continues to house a portion of the Gilmore Automobile Museum. The area known as the Todd Farm remains a wildlife sanctuary where thousands of visitors thrill to the sight of vast flocks of wild geese and herds of deer browsing on the old mint fields.

When Hiawatha
Came to Petoskey

It was as if the billowing curtain of time had parted when Hiawatha lifted the wigwam flap and stepped forth in full Ojibwa splendor. Finely wrought beadwork decorated his fringed buckskin tunic, leggings and moccasins and an eagle feather headdress covered his long black braids.

Hiawatha strode to the waiting birch bark canoe, pushed off and with a few graceful paddle strokes glided silently across the water:

"Forth upon the Gitche Gumee,
On the shinning Big-Sea-Water,
With his fishing line of cedar,
Of the twisted bark of cedar,
Forth to catch the sturgeon Nahma,
Mishe-Nahma, King of Fishes,
In his birch canoe exulting
All alone went Hiawatha."

Then, just as quickly as it had fluffed open time's curtain clapped shut as a crowd of spectators packed upon bleachers on the opposite side of the little bay broke out in discordant applause. None among their number clapped more appreciately then Longfellow. No, not Henry Wadsworth Longfellow, who had penned the Indian epic, but his daughter Alice.

The year was 1905 and that summer a company of Chippewa actors had journeyed from their Garden River, Ontario, reservation to perform the first of a series of Hiawatha pageants that would delight audiences over the succeeding ten years. The Grand Rapids and Indiana Railroad staged those performances, not on the shores of Gitchee Gumee,

This Chippewa actor from Garden River, Ontario, played Hiawatha in the Petoskey pageant.

better known as Lake Superior, but at their new park Wa-ya-ga-mug on Round Lake, north of Petoskey midway between Conway and the celebrated Methodist resort of Bay View.

That the heroic poem based on the legends of the Chippewa (or Ojibway a varient of the same tribe) was actually set, as Longfellow had acknowledged, "on the southern shore of Lake Superior, in the region between the Pictured Rocks and the Grand Sable" did not bother Longfellow's daughter, who after watching the play for a solid week thought "it possessed an indescribable charm," or few if any of the hordes who watched the "creditable spectacular exhibition as a truthful representation of the Indian as a romantic figure." Fewer still minded the incongruity of the name of the saga's heroic figure.

Longfellow had substituted Hiawatha for his original title, Manabozho, the earthly messenger of the Gitchee Manitou who figured prominently in Ojibway mythology. Hiawatha was a totally different hero from Iroquois mythology. That the Iroquois or the Ojibway had been traditional enemies for centuries, slaughtering each other with savage passion, seemed not to have troubled the poet. How the Upper Peninsula, the ancestral domain of the Ojibway, came to proudly proclaim itself "the land of Hiawatha" is a saga of poetic license made to run the gauntlet.

The story begins in 1822 with the arrival in Sault Ste. Marie of a young geologist named Henry Rowe Schoolcraft. He had first seen the Lake Superior country two years before as a member of the exploring expedition led by Michigan Territorial Governor Lewis Cass. In part because of the friendship that blossomed between the two during that arduous canoe trip Schoolcraft was appointed Indian agent for the Upper Great Lakes with headquarters at the Sault. That he knew little about Indian culture and spoke no Indian language was apparently of little concern to the government. Nevertheless upon arriving at the ancient village couched at the foot of the roaring rapids Schoolcraft launched a study of the Indian that would become his life's work.

When he arrived at his new post in 1822, Schoolcraft had the good fortune to board with the John Johnston family. Johnston, then known as "the patriarch of the Sault" had been born in Ireland in 1762. At the age of 18 he immigrated to Montreal. Three years later he came to the Sault where he conducted a lucrative fur trading operation. He married a remarkable Indian woman, renamed Susan, the daughter of an influential Chippewa chief and renowned story teller, Waub Ojeg of La Pointe, Wisconsin. At their house in the Sault, the Johnstons created an oasis of culture on the frontier. Their many children received an excellent education, studying the classics at home and attending private schools in Canada for finishing. Susan also acculturated them in the language, customs and lore of her people.

Welcomed into their society, Schoolcraft became a fast friend of the Johnstons. He recorded in his private journal on July 28, 1822: "I have in fact stumbled, as it were, on the only family in Northwest America who could in Indian lore have acted as my guide, philosopher and friend." The following year he married their beautiful daughter, Jane, "the northern Pocahontas."

In particular, the Johnston family assisted Schoolcraft in collecting, translating and interpreting the oral myths of the Chippewa, known as lodge stories. As the daughter of a celebrated chief, Susan provided many important contacts and Jane and her brother George proved invaluable as translators. Because of the unique opportunities afforded him via the Johnstons Schoolcraft focused much of his attention on the preservation and promotion of the oral myths of the Chippewa.

He first published four of those lodge stories in his *Travels in the Central Portion of the Mississippi Valley* (1825) and others in a manuscript magazine he compiled and circulated at the Sault during the winter of 1826-27. In the 1830s Chandler Robbins Gilman and Anna Jameson included some of the stories Schoolcraft had collected in their travel narratives about the north country.

Then in 1839 Schoolcraft published his two volume collection of Chippewa tales, *Algic Researches.* It contained many of the original stories that would serve as the basis for *The Song of Hiawatha* including: Manabozho, Mon-Dau-Min or the Origin of Indian Corn, Pays-Puk-Keewiss and Kwasind or the fearfully strong man, While not a popular success - one small edition satisfied the market demand - the volumes brought Schoolcraft scholarly accolades.

Schoolcraft published additional Chippewa legends in *Oneota, or the Red Race of America* (1844-45) and in the six volumes of his massive magnum opus, *Historical and Statistical Information Respecting the History, Conditions and Prospects of the Indian Tribes of the United States* (1851-57).

One reader, in particular, found Schoolcraft's Indian legends of intriguing interest - Henry Wadsworth Longfellow. He wrote: "I pored over Mr. Schoolcraft's writings nearly three years, before I resolved to appropriate something of them to my own use." In 1854 the 37-year-old poet with more than a dozen published volumes resigned his professorship at Harvard and began writing at his home in Cambridge, Mass., the epic Indian saga. He first titled the work *Manabozho* but later, for some arcane reason, switched to *Hiawatha,* an Iroquois demigod credited with forming the five tribes into the Iroquois League in the 16th century. Although in all fairness some

Iroquois storytellers, themselves, have confused Hiawatha's exploits with those of another of their mythic characters, Teharonhiawakhon, who was somewhat analogous to the Ojibway Manabozho.

In any event, Longfellow published his masterpiece in November 1855, and it became an overnight sensation - selling 50,000 copies within 15 months. The following year Schoolcraft rushed into print a revised edition of Algic Researches which he titled *The Myth of Hiawatha...* in an attempt to piggyback on Longfellow's phenomenal success. Unfortunately, once again, a single edition satisfied the public's desire to read the genuine Indian stories Schoolcraft had assembled

But *The Song of Hiawatha's* popularity continued to grow despite allegations by some critics, including rival poet Edgar Allen Poe, that Longfellow had plagairized the plot and poetic measure from the ancient Finnish epic, *The Kalevala.* Within a few months of the volume's appearance audiences were being regaled by dramatic readings of the poem, stage plays based on its plot appeared and across the nation place names, steamboats, chewing tobacco and other products had begun to bear the names of Hiawatha, Minnehaha and other of the poem's characters.

Americans continued to be fascinated with the poem that the 19th Century chronicler of poets, Edmund C. Stedman, termed "the one poem that beguiles the reader to see the birch and ash, the heron and eagle and deer, as they seem to the red man himself, and to join for the moment in his simple creed and wonderment." That fascination and a turn-of-the-century "back to nature" movement inspired the Grand Rapids and Indiana Railroad to harvest some tourist dollars at the resort it platted on Round Lake. There, on a wooded point that juts out into the lake, they constructed an Indian village as the scene of the play. Across a little landlocked bay rose the

A scene from the Hiawatha pagant enacted at Round Lake.

spectator's grandstand.

The resort owners thought the site a fitting one because, according to their promotional literature, it was:

"the very place where the Indian of the old days camped when it blew hard on the Great Lakes; he could always get a deer, a bass or a dore [an archaic name for walleye pike] - a favorite food of his; here he had suitable soil and climate for his corn, beans and potatoes, here he grew the bark for his canoe covering, the cedar and all the roots necessary for construction; here his innate love for the beautiful was satisfied, and here in defense of it all the Ojibways and Ottawas fought the Iroquois."

Despite that admission of the tribes' long standing enmity, the nagging fact that Hiawatha was Iroquois seems not to have distressed the railroad promoters, the thousands of spectators or the Indian actors.

By the season of 1906 the railroad had added other attractions. Visitors might stay in "new clean Indian wigwams" thereby "arresting physical degeneracy and permitting the strong to enjoy and preserve their strength and make the weak strong by moderate and carefully administered exercise in open air life." They could compete in water polo, swimming matches and tilting contests in the lake, take woodcraft classes, visit the Indian museum complete with "live Indians," enjoy "sun baths, sand baths, clay baths and water baths," listen to out of doors lecturers, paddle in sunset canoe parties or simply be pulled in a canoe behind a motor boat. A central dining hall for the back-to-nature campers specialized in fish breakfasts. In case the Indian theme began to cloy the railroad took the precaution of providing an

Eskimo igloo with its native occupants and a tea house where kimono clad Japanese offered rice cakes and other "varied amusements."

For ten summers the Hiawatha pageant at Wa-Ya-Ga-Mug regaled thousands of refugees from Chicago and elsewhere. The director, a Mr. Armstrong from Montreal, integrated local Ottawa into the cast and other Grand Traverse region Indians conducted craft workshops and sold baskets, leather work and other traditional products. Local entrepreneurs also developed products catering to the tourist market. Area gift shops offered plates, bud vases, creamers and other ceramic souvenirs picturing scenes from the play. In 1911 Rand McNally and Company published a handsome "Player's Edition" of *The Song of Hiawatha,* illustrated with photographs of Wa-Ya-Ga-Mug and the Indian actors.

But competion from other attractions catering to the burgeoning north country tourist industry brought about the demise of the Hiawatha plays at Round Lake just prior to World War I. By then the Upper Peninsula had firmly established itself via promotional literature and other media as "the land of Hiawatha"

And the next time those majestic twin harps of steel convey you high above the Straits of Mackinac to the magic Upper Peninsula you might contemplate Nokomis, Minnehaha and - Manabozho.

The Wizard of Oz
at Macatawa Park

Lyman Frank Baum, the prolific children's author best remembered for his American classic, *The Wonderful Wizard of Oz*, enjoyed a productive year in 1907. That summer at his cottage in Macatawa Park, a fashionable resort near Holland, Michigan, he completed his second sequel to Dorothy's adventures in the land of Munchkins and flying monkeys. Eager readers across America would be thrilled to find the lavishly illustrated *Ozma of Oz* beneath the Christmas tree that year.

Baum also found time in 1907 to pen the plays " Down Missouri Way" and "Our Mary" and a poem about the Michigan resort he loved so well, "To Macatawa," which appeared in the Grand Rapids *Sunday Herald* on September 1st:

"Happy the boy or girl who knows
This land of rainbows, beaux and bows,
Where every night there is a chance
To revel in the merry dance;
Where motor boats are thick as bees
And all can note whene'er they please;
Where all is love and peace and Joy
Without a 'skeeter to annoy
Or sign of any carking care
To be discovered anywhere."

Using two of the half dozen pseudonyms under which he cranked out long series of juvenile novels, Baum also published that year Laura Bancroft's *Policeman Bluejay* and Capt. Hugh Fitzgerald's *Sam Steel's Adventures in Panama*.

Perhaps most significant for Michigan's literary history, 1907 saw the publication, in a small privately printed edition, of Baum's *Tamawaca Folks*. He issued the book under the penname John Estes Cooke, an esoteric variation of the 19th century Virginian novelist and historian, John Esten Cooke. *Tamawaca* (anagram for Macatawa) *Folks*, the first novel to be set in the Holland area, although little known except to rare book dealers and Baum devotees, is a charming love story intertwined with a plot based on an interesting series of actual happenings.

While not of the classic stature of Baum's *Wizard of Oz*, the first original American fairy tale, it is, nonetheless, well worth reading. Consider Baum's description of the beach at Macatawa that continues to draw thousands of recreationists yearly:

> A few paces more brought them to a magnificent view of the great inland sea, and soon they emerged upon a broad beach lapped by the rolling waves of grand old Michigan. Jarrod's (the main character of the novel who is being sold a cottage) eyes sparkled. It was beautiful at this point, he was forced to admit, and the cool breath of the breeze that swept over the water sent an exhilarating vigor to the bottom of his lungs and bought a sudden glow to his cheek...

The picturesque sand dunes at the mouth of the Black River and the miles of dazzling white beaches stretching along Lake Michigan about which Baum rhapsodized in *Tamawaca Folks* had begun attracting vacationers as early as the 1870s. Holland newspapers of the decade carried accounts of camping and fishing parties from Chicago, Grand Rapids and elsewhere. The exploitation of the recreational possibilities to be found where the Allegan and Ottawa County line touched Lake Michigan began in earnest in August 1881, when an association of Holland citizens purchased land on the south side of the mouth of the Black River. Macatawa (an Ottawa word meaning black in reference to the darkness of the waters of the Black River) Park was soon planned, lots sold, fashionable Italianate, Romanesque and Queen Anne cottages erected, and by the end of the year, three hotels welcomed guests. In 1895, the resort's most luxurious hostelry, The Hotel Macatawa, an enormous Queen Anne structure wrapped with two-story verandas, was constructed.

The resort had a particular attraction for Chicagoans and in 1899, Baum, then a resident of the Windy City, first visited Macatawa. His career up to then had been eclectic. Born in Chittenango, New York, in 1856, he grew up in a wealthy, pampered environment. Because a congenital heart problem prevented him from playing rough games with other children, he instead found refuge in books, romantic Victorian novels and fairy tales in particular.

In the 1870s and early 1880s, Baum followed his first love, the theater, working as an actor and playwright. His marriage to Maude Gage in 1882 and the subsequent birth of two sons forced him to leave the stage for a more dependable livelihood. He tried a hodgepodge of occupations including marketing Baum's Castorine, an axle lubricant, and raising exotic breeds of chickens. His first book published in 1886 was a treatise on chickens.

The year 1888 found the Baum family in the frontier settlement of Aberdeen, Dakota Territory. There he operated a "5 & 10 Cent Store" called Baum's Bazaar. When that enterprise failed, he turned to editing the Aberdeen *Saturday Pioneer*, where he further honed his writing skills. A cyclone that ripped through Aberdeen in 1890 undoubtedly inspired the prairie twister that carried Dorothy to Munchkin Land in Baum's first Oz book.

When his newspaper went bankrupt in 1891,

the Baum family retreated back east to Chicago. Baum wrote for the Chicago *Evening Post* for a spell, tried his hand as a traveling crockery salesman and in 1897 became editor of a pioneer journal for show window dressers.

In 1897, Baum published his first juvenile book, *Mother Goose in Prose,* an adaption of old nursery rhymes to current themes. Two years later he teamed up with William W. Denslow, a talented young artist, to produce a second series of fables. *Father Goose, His Book* became the best selling juvenile volume of 1899.

Royalties from *Father Goose* and the even more successful, *The Wonderful Wizard of Oz,* that appeared the following year allowed the Baum family the luxury of summering at Macatawa Park, which Baum called his "imitation paradise." Baum, incidently, coined OZ when he spied the alphabetical label on the bottom drawer of a file cabinet, 'O-Z."

As the royalty checks continued to flow from his New York and Chicago publishers, in 1902 Baum purchased a rambling cottage in Macatawa, overlooking Lake Michigan. He named it "The Sign of the Goose" in honor of the source of much of its purchase price, his *Father Goose* book. Baum further commemorated his first successful book by applying the goose motif throughout the cottage, including stained glass window depicting a white goose in a green background, geese stencils on the wall borders and handcrafted oak furniture decorated with geese.

While enjoying the pristine Lake Michigan view and its stimulating breezes at "The Sign of the Goose" Baum hatched the plots for and wrote some if not all of two of his sequels to *The Wonderful Wizard of Oz.* In his first sequel, *The Marvelous Land of Oz,* published in 1904,a new character, professor H. M. Woggle-Bug, replaced Dorothy in the leading role. He had gotten the inspiration for that character,

"HELP, HELP!" SCREAMED THE KING

John R. Neill's illustrations brightened Baum's *Ozma of Oz* book.

according to a biography of Baum co-authored by his son Frank in 1961, when while he was walking the beach at Macatawa, a little girl held up a curious insect and asked Baum what it was. " A Woggle-Bug," he told her. Her delight with the name was second only to Baum's.

Baum signed the author's note to his second Oz sequel, *Ozma of Oz*, "Macatawa, 1907." Dorothy Gale, the Kansas farm girl, returned to the plot of this book. But Toto stayed in Kansas with Auntie Em, while Dorothy made a voyage to Europe with her Uncle Henry. En route Dorothy was swept overboard in a wooden chicken coop with a talking hen named Billina. After the coop washed up on the shore of a strange land, Dorothy would link up with her old friends, the three musketeers of Oz, Tinman, Scarecrow, and Cowardly Lion, and a variety of new characters, including the benevolent and beautiful Queen of Oz, Ozma, Ticktok, the machine man; the hungry tiger and the King of Ev. Billina's special skills came in handy when Dorothy encountered the evil-tempered Nomes, whose only fear was freshly laid eggs.

Baum's *Tamawaca Folks*, however, was a "horse of a different color." It documented in thinly veiled characterizations the true story of how a coterie of cottagers wrested back control of the Macatawa Association from two unscrupulous entrepreneurs. Over the years the pair had usurped the public domain there and the lucrative concessions which amounted to a virtual monopoly over groceries, laundry, ferry service, etc. Baum described one of the pair as a "fine old religious duffer, who loves to pray for your spiritual welfare while he feels for your pockets," a type only too familiar to Holland area residents. Baum also made a tongue in cheek reference to himself when he had the other of the scoundrels point out: "the cottage of our distinguished author. Don't have to work, you know. Just writes books and people buy'em. Snap, ain't it?" The actual facts behind the successful outcome of the Macatawa Association's rebirth can be traced in a September 1, 1907 Grand Rapids *Sunday Herald* feature story on Macatawa as well as the original minute books and other records of the association which are preserved in the Joint Archives of Holland at Hope College.

Baum served as one of the directors of the Macatawa Association which succeeded in regaining the property owner's rights to the resort. Officers of the association and its predecessor, The Macatawa Park Cottagers Association, frequently met at "The Sign of the Goose." Baum was also a member of the Macatawa Bay Yacht Club. Each year for a decade, as soon as the Chicago schools let out, Baum and his family, which had grown to four boys, spent the entire summer at Macatawa.

A dapper, moustached, little man, who though forbidden to smoke because of his heart condition, often chewed on a large unlighted cigar, Baum was remembered by Macatawans not so much for his appearance as for his talent for story telling. During a visit to "The Sign of the Goose," the Chicago poet Eunice Tietjens asked Baum why he never lighted his cigar. "Oh, I only do so when I go swimming," he replied. "You see," he explained gravely, "I can't swim, so when the cigar goes out I know I'm getting over my depth." Then he lighted the cigar and walked into Lake Michigan until it was extinguished. "There now, Baum said upon returning to the beach, "if it hadn't been for the cigar I would have drowned." Needless to say, the children of Macatawa, of all ages, loved to listen to the magical stories he concocted about almost everything.

In 1909, possibly as a result of a burglary of his boathouse, Baum sold his property at Macatawa and moved to Palm Springs, California. The "Sign of the

Goose" burned to the ground during the summer of 1927. The man who won fame as "the Royal Historian of Oz" died of a stroke in 1919. But America's love affair with the Land of Oz and its characters, heightened by the 1939 technicolor extravaganza starring Judy Garland, continues as strong as ever.

Fittingly, in 1988 and 1989, some surviving members of the original Munchkins from the 1939 movie, traveled to Macatawa to participate in the annual Oz Festival. And better yet, it is still possible to relive life at Macatawa during the Baum era, as seen through the "Wizard's" own eyes, in the pages of *Tamawaca Folks*.

The Atlantic City
of the West

Black plumes billowing from its twin stacks, *The City of South Haven* sliced through the whitecaps at the mouth of the Van Buren County harbor whose name she bore. Nicknamed "The White Flyer" in honor of her speed of 20 miles per hour, the 248 feet long steamer was the pride of the Chicago-South Haven Line.

That sultry July Saturday in 1908 nearly 2,500 heat-wracked, work-jaded and nerve-jangled Chicagoans had hurried up the big ship's gang plank at her dock at the north end of the Rush Street Bridge. Now after a bracing five hour cruise across the big lake, the gaily dressed wasp-waisted women and straw-hatted men crowded the triple deck railings to catch their first glimpse of "The Atlantic City of the West."

It was an era when South Haven boasted a reputation as a resort mecca *par excellence* - when the promotional phrase, "Michigan in the Summer," packed thousand upon thousands of vacationists, chiefly Chicago citizens, upon great floating palaces named *The Iroquois, The Theodore Roosevelt, The Petoskey, The City of Kalamazoo, The City of South Haven* and the ill fated *Eastland*. Those big ships once proudly steamed past the same lighthouse that continues to stand sentinel at the end of the south pier.

What harried Windy City hog butcher, tool maker, stacker of wheat, player with railroads or nation's freight handler could resist the likes of the promotional literature that rhetorically queried:

Would you dip leisurely into the lapping ripples of that great inland ocean, Lake Michigan, or ride the

The City of South Haven laden with vacationists.

surf on the dashing waves of its mighty waters rolled high by western winds? Would you bask in the sunlight of pastoral scenes, catch fragrant whiffs of peach blossoms, build up strength and vigor with health giving fruits and vegetables, new laid eggs, rich pure milk? Would you spend a vacation full to overflowing with your favorite pursuits, golfing, tennis, yachting, motor boating, tramping in the great dune lands?

No matter that July was too late for the whiff of peach blossoms - South Haven stood ready and eager to provide the rest of those allurements and more.

In 1898, local Congregational flock leader, the Rev. Charles D. Brower, traced the origins of the city's resort industry to a summer about twelve years before when Mrs. Henry M. Avery "entertained friends who were so pleased with the place and people as to return another season with others. The house was enlarged, then another built, to accommodate the visitors."

Sniffing money in the westerly lake breezes other South Havenites soon opened their homes to guests. Many built structures specifically to house the growing numbers of tourists. In the summer of 1896, some 40,000 passengers arrived in South Haven by rail and steamship. Six years later South Haven claimed more than 215 resorts, hotels and rooming houses. By 1913, an estimated 100,000 visitors would "come and go each season."

Long lines of horse-drawn drays queued up along the dock to convey the hundreds who streamed off the big ships to their respective lodgings. Gasoline powered launches pulled barges crammed with excursionists to additional hostelries and parks situated as far as five miles up the Black River.

Among the largest and finest of South Haven's resorts was the Avery Beach Hotel, a rambling Queen

Anne monstrosity wrapped with multi-storied porches that stood just north of the North Beach. When the massive structure and seven nearby cottages burned in 1907 local entrepreneurs lost little time in dreaming up grandiose replacements. One such project that made a big splash in Chicago newspapers in 1908 featured a dome-topped concrete, fire-proof hotel at the Avery site. From the new hotel a pier would extend 1,200 feet out into the lake, terminating in a dancing pavilion and a dock for the big steamers. But the highlight of prestigious Chicago architect George W. Maher's proposal was the construction of a fifty foot wide boardwalk, elevated eight feet high and stretching from the drawbridge over the Black River along the north bank of the channel and then making a great bow to link up with the new hotel's pier. Exuberant promoters envisioned South Haven becoming the "Atlantic City of the West" replete with the wicker rolling chairs popular at the New Jersey resort. They could all but taste Michigan's version of salt water taffy.

But as 1908 gave way to 1909 followed by two more years without the first board laid for the grand walkway they were forced to trim their sails a bit. Then in 1912 a small army of carpenters began hammering together the Avery Beach Casino, a huge pavilion resembled an athletic field house decorated with towers at its four corners. When completed the following year it comprised one of the largest dance halls in the nation, its gaudy interior illuminated by more than 2,000 electric light bulbs in various colors.

At the big casino on summer evenings hundreds of couples turkey trotted and tangoed. They performed the Castle Walk, the Boston Dip, the Hesitation Waltz, the Flying Two Step. They did the Bunny Hug, the Grizzly Bear and other popular dances of the era to the strains of some of the country's most famous big bands including those of

Kalamazoo's own, Charles L. Fischer, "the man with the million dollar smile." Revelers whose feet had not gotten enough at the big pavilion could board ship for "The Saturday Evening Mid-Lake Frolic" and continue to turn, dip, whirl and corte all the way back to Chicago.

And there was plenty else to do in South Haven during this golden era of its resort industry. Tourists might enjoy six precarious rides for a quarter on the big figure eight roller coaster that stood near the present site of the Michigan Maritime Museum. They could imbibe culture at the local Opera House where touring companies intoned melodious if incomprehensible lyrics.

Beginning in 1908 they could watch flickering silent movies at the OK Theatre on Phoenix Street and later the rival Princess Theatre and the Bullfrog Theatre. They might spin around the roller skating rink at the foot of Broadway, watch in awe as the surfmen at the Life Saving Station blasted their breeches buoy cannon at targets or, beginning in 1909, tee off at the city's original golf course near the present Michigan State Police Post.

One now prevalent South Haven attraction was noticeably absent. Those who relished alcoholic refreshments needed to smuggle their booze into town in wicker picnic baskets and portmanteaux. Decades before the Volstead Act ushered in national prohibition Van Buren County teetotalers had taken advantage of Michigan's local option law to vote themselves as dry as the nearby sand dunes. "The crime, the pauperism, the wrecked homes, the bleeding hearts and the grinding taxes which follow in the wake of the liquor traffic are unknown among us," the Rev. William H. Millar was happy to sermonize in a 1896 promotional tract.

Parched vacationists needed to content themselves to bellying up to the ornate marble bars of

Abell's Drug Store on Phoenix Street or Van Ostrand's Drug Store on Center Street. The latter, one of the region's most opulent establishments, featured a white-jacketed crew of four who jerked countless sodas, phosphates and fizzes.

The demise of the glorious era when the pleasure arks floated their great loads of human cargo to South Haven's booming resorts began in the dark days of the Great Depression. The increasing availability of automotive travel made further inroads on ship traffic. The Avery Casino continued to draw crowds until fire claimed it in 1937. By that year, most South Haven promoters had quietly dropped their references to "The Atlantic City of the West," a title they had prematurely adopted and stubbornly clung to despite the original boardwalk fiasco.

Not until the 1990s would a more modest version of the boardwalk projected in 1908 grace the opposite bank of the channel. The wicker rolling chairs and salt water taffy are yet to come.

Culture Under Canvas
in Paw Paw

"Come to Paw Paw, come to Maple Lake, come to the Chautauqua!" trumpeted Henry E. Shaefer, Paw Paw nurseryman and local manager of the community's Chautauqua. The year was 1910, the golden era of the traveling tent Chautauqua's modeled after what had started in the 1870s as a summer camp for Sunday school teachers on the shores of Lake Chautauqua in southwestern New York.

The traveling Chautauquas that arrived in hundreds of midwestern cities and towns each summer had evolved into a uniquely American institution, fondly remembered as "culture under canvas." Week long programs staged under the big top featured inspirational speakers, orchrestras, singers, opera, plays, humorists and a host of other entertaining and uplifting attractions that gave millions of rural residents their first taste of the cultural opportunities formerly enjoyed only in the big cities of the east.

Many Michigan communities hosted Chautauquas, but few did so with the aplomb of Paw Paw. The Van Buren County seat had presented its first Chautauqua in 1909 and the success of that endeavor had spurred the citizens of "the Maple City," a civic hyperbole coined in honor of the many maple trees that lined the village streets, to go all out for a nine day long Chautauqua extravaganza on August 20-28, 1910.

The gala event would be held in a beautiful maple grove known as Thayer's Lake View, situated in the heart of the village on the shores of Maple Lake. That lake, incidently, had emerged but two years earlier, a by-product of a power dam on the Paw Paw River. Nevertheless, local entrepreneurs had hastened to capitalize on its potential as a resort industry, constructing fashionable cottages along its banks and platting numerous recreational grounds.

While Paw Paw's entire population numbered but 1,643 persons in 1910, the Maple Lake Chautauqua Association confidently expected to draw enough patrons from surrounding Van Buren County to fill the giant tent capable of seating 3,000 the Midland Chautauqua Circuit, headquartered in Des Moines, Iowa, would pitch at Thayer's grove.

Enterprising citizens converted their houses into tourists homes, economical forerunners of today's pricey "bed and breakfasts," to accommodate the Chautauqua throngs. Equally "wide awake" Paw Paw merchants advertized spin off products such as the Bennett & Lake Furniture and Undertaking establishment's "Chautauqua reed rockers" at $1.98.

Chautauqau promoters promised a program that would be "one of the strongest and best that has ever been offered in the great state of Michigan, and includes besides lectures of national fame, music and other features the very best which genius can devise or money procure." And if that were not enough to lure culture seekers to Paw Paw the price of admittance was ridiculously low even by 1910 standards. Adults could attend all 34 sessions held during the nine days by purchasing a season ticket for $2.00 - children from seven to 13 years old paid but $1.00 and those under seven were admitted free. Single admission tickets cost 25 cents.

By the afternoon of Saturday, August 20, an army of roustabouts had raised the enormous tent on the shore of Maple Lake and thousands of Van Buren County citizens eager for culture had crowded within. The Chautauqua began at 2:30 with the DeKoven Male Quartet "singing many of the old songs and singing them well." Following that Austrian born Dr. E.A. Steiner lectured on immigration, a "social

The Hugh Anderson Operatic Company cast appeared at the 1917 Paw Paw Chautauqua.

problem" them troubling many Americans. In the evening the DeKoven singers returned to the stage, and Dr. James Headley, "one of princes of the American platform" delivered a 100 minute long lecture "which straitened the hearts of all with a desire to do better and to live better and to move out on a higher plane." No lightweight audience those Paw Paw Chautauquans.

An so it went over the following eight days, a cosmopolitan feast of music and singing by the African-American Midland Jubilee Singers, the Royal Hungarian Orchestra and the Imperial Ladies' Band which hailed from Reading in Hillsdale County. Miss Rita Rich sang folk songs from around the world and Miss Rose Marie Nusbaum performed character songs from England, Scotland and Germany.

On Monday Paw Paw listened in spellbound horror as Mrs. Florence E. Maybrick related how she was unjustly convicted of poisoning her aristocratic English husband, stripped of her fortune, and torn from her children while she suffered 15 years of imprisonment in a British gaol. On Tuesday New York City attorney Walter M. Chandler spoke on "The Trial of Jesus from a Lawyer's Standpoint." Wednesday brought nationally popular comedian Everett Kemp, "just to hear Kemp laugh is worth the price."

A roster of other speakers lectured on more serious and uplifting themes. Their names conjure up W.C. Fields characters: Sen. J.P. Dolliver, Dr. J. Everest Cathell, Rev. Homer C. Stuntz, Prof. Lucian Follansbee; and many decades before Mohammad Ali achieved fistic prominence an Indian by the same name lectured to Paw Paw on his country's mysteries.

The highlight of the entire Chautauqua, however, came on Friday afternoon when William Jennings Bryan stepped to the podium. A Democratic political leader from Nebraska revered as "the Great

Commoner" because of his appeal to the ordinary working man, Bryan had run for the presidency three times to be successively beaten by McKinley, Roosevelt and Taft. Despite his political misfortunes he was also an indomitable Chautauqua speaker, delivering moving, if relatively meaningless, speeches to hundreds of audiences each Chautauqua season. In the heat of the summer he appeared on stage armed with a big palm leaf fan and a block of ice. During his fiery speech he rested his hand on the block and as his bald head began to glow red, he gave it cooling caresses with his icy palm.

By Sunday evening when Denton C. Crowl, "The Protrayalist," who would now be termed an impersonator, had appeared as the last act of the great Paw Paw Chautauqua of 1910, the Van Buren County audience had gotten more than its fill of culture. Hundreds filed out of the big tent, made their weary way home by buckboard and horse to return to the more down to earth concerns of the workaday world.

But when August 1911 rolled around Paw Paw was prepared to do it again. That years' nine day Chautauqua featured such headlines as comic impersonator Ellsworth Plumstead, the Fiechtl Tyrolean Alpine Yodelers, Salvator Ciricillo's Italian Band, a family of New Zeeland aborigines who lectured on "From Savagery to Civilization" and Prof. Pamahasika and his trained birds, dogs and monkeys.

The Hon. Horatio "Goodroads" Earle, Michigan's first Highway Department director, held a session to drum up support for his hard fought campaign to better the state's notoriously abominable road system. Ironically, it was improved roads coupled with the increasing prevalence of the automobiles, motion pictures and the advent of radio that spelled doom for the tent Chautauqua concept.

Paw Paw continued to host Chautauquas on

the shores of Maple Lake for several more seasons. By 1917 and America's entry into WW I the event had taken on a decidedly military theme and been reduced to seven days. Promoters of that year's special "Junior Chautauqua" geared toward children promised parents "new ways of having fun - new games - and they will probably play 'Soldier' and drill just like 'real soldiers' - Won't that be fun?"

Paw Paw's Chautauqua did not survive the "roaring 20s." Although the pitching of the big tent on the shore of Maple Lake no longer highlighted each summer, glorious memories of exotic acts, strains of beautiful music and morally uplifting orators would remain vibrant for many more decades.

Pigeoners' Lament

Old Simon Pokagon, chief of the Pokagon band of Potawatomi and known as "the best educated full-bloodied Indian of his time," sat at his desk working on an essay. His sad, wrinkled face relaxed and his black eyes glistened as he leaned back in his chair and thought of the vast flocks of "O-me-me-wog," passenger pigeons, he had watched so many times flowing across the Michigan sky for hours on end, like a great rainbow river.

Then he dipped his pen in ink and wrote: "It was proverbial with our fathers that if the Great Spirit in His wisdom could have created a more elegant bird in plumage, form and movement, he never did." Pokagon published his essay on passenger pigeons in the November, 1895, issue of the *Chautauquan Magazine*. Living near the Van Buren County community Hartford then, the old chief would soon move to Lee Township, Allegan County, where he died in 1899.

By that date those wild pigeons he so loved, that were twice the size of a mourning dove with iridescent blue plumage, red breasts and brilliant orange eyes, had all but dissappeared from his native state. Mercifully, Pokagon did not live to see the last passenger pigeon on earth die in a Cincinnati Zoo in 1914.

All that remained were a few stuffed specimens and the bitter-sweet recollections of the pioneers, sportsmen and professional "pigeoners" who hounded the avian bounty to extinction.

In 1914, ironically, C.H. Hall, a pioneer from the Saugatuck vicinity, told western Allegan County historian Henry H. Hutchinson: "When the pigeons were migrating the flocks were so dense that they would cast a shadow on the ground, and were almost sufficient to hide the sun."

Hall also recalled how he and neighboring settlers cut down trees filled with nests to get at the tender "butterball squabs," harvesting from 40 to 50 of the nestlings from a single tree. Contenting themselves with the many barrels of squabs they pickled in brine for future use, the parent birds were allowed to live to nest again.

Not so selective, however, were the professional pigeoners who made a lucrative livlihood by following the migrating flocks. Their favored method was to lure a flock of pigeons in with a blinded bird known as a stool pigeon and then trap as many as 1,000 at a time in huge clap nets. Hall described their techniques:

They would strew grain on the ground, tie a few birds to stakes, and pull a string attached to the stool pigeon to make him flutter and attract the flock that was flying over. When the ground was well covered with birds they would trip the net by pulling another string, the net being so arranged that it would fly over and cover the lot. The trapper concealed himself under a booth made of green bush. The birds were killed by pinching their heads, were packed in barrels without dressing, and shipped to market.

Other southwestern Michigan hunters used varied methods. Sullivan Cook, who homesteaded in eastern Cass County, never forgot the spring morning in 1854 when his 12-year-old daughter came runnning in, exclaiming: "Pa, come out and see the pigeons!" He looked out the door to see flock after flock of the birds skimming low over his fields. He grabbed his bouble barreled muzzle loader, a powder flask and shot pouch and running to the center of a five acre field began blasting away. He brought down from three to 15 with each shot. Within a short time, his daughter had collected 276 pigeons. After breakfast,

Pigeoners lured luckless birds with salt and stool pigeons.

Cook hitched up his team and hauled the birds the ten miles to Three Rivers where he soon sold them for 65 cents a dozen. Returning home, he felt "well satisfied with my day's work."

On the other hand, H.H. Goodrich, who settled near New Richmond, Allegan County, in 1844, remembered his uncle using a technique that saved even the expense of amunition. He merely stood on the brow of a hill and batted the birds down with a club as they flew by. Pokagon wrote in disgust of another old hunter who caught hundreds of pigeons by getting them drunk on whiskey soaked grain.

Even those imaginative hunting methods had seemingly no appreciable effect on the massive flocks that sometimes broke down entire forests under their combined weight when nesting. With many natural predators such as hawks, owls, raccoons, foxes and snakes in addition to man the birds needed to maintain a huge breeding population. Then too, natural calamities like sudden ice storms off of Lake Michigan might claim millions of victims. Despite those ancient threats it was the unregulated wholesale slaughter for profit practiced by the many of pigeoners that spelled their doom.

Shelby, a hamlet situated along the railroad on the Oceana County frontier, was facing bleak times in 1874. It looked to the locals like it might join the ranks of many similar communities that became ghost towns. But that spring occurred "the most singular event in the history of the county." An enormous flock of pigeons selected a section of the woods a few miles from the village as a nesting ground. Within days every train from the south brought a growing army of pigeoners. The local economy boomed as citizens built barrels and coops, sold supplies and boarded the hunters. An even larger nesting in 1876 gave Shelby a national reputation as the "locality of the greatest pigeon roost in the U.S." More than 500 "strangers" found shelter in Shelby that spring and in excess of 700,000 birds were shipped by train alone. That "golden shower" at the pigeon's expense "placed the village squarely on its feet."

An even bigger avian bonanza ocurred in Hartford in 1870. Having moved from Cass County to Van Buren County Cook witnessed the work of a coterie of local pigeoners who discovered an immense pigeon roost nearby. Some hunters took as many as 6,000 birds in one day. Throughout the 40 day period trains loaded with an average of 300,000 pigeons - 12 million dead birds in all - chugged out of Hartford daily for eastern markets.

Small wonder that Cook ended his account of the tragedy he published in *Forest and Stream* in 1903 thusly: "My young friends, I want to humbly ask your forgivness for having taken a small part in the destruction of this, the most exciting of sport. And there is not one of us but is ashamed of the slaughter which has robbed you of enjoyment."

Chevrolet Drove
The Cornelian Car

Howard E. Blood, a young mechanic from Allegan, stood in the pits at Indianapolis, oblivious to everything but the knot of race cars roaring down the brick straight away. It was Memorial Day, 1915. He squeezed the wrenches he held in either hand until his knuckles stood out white when he saw it, No. 27, a little white speedster, low slung and weighing only 900 pounds, an automotive David amongst the Dusenbergs, Peugeots, Mercedes, Bugattis, and other Goliaths of the track.

Blood had designed, built and proudly named the Cornelian car after either his Aunt Cornelia, Cornell University or both. And now with famed driver Louis Chevrolet at the wheel his little creation raced in the spotlight before the entire automotive world.

Chevrolet had souped up its four cylinder Sterling engine to 116 cubic inches and qualified the Cornelian at 81.1 miles an hour, tenths of a second behind a 300 cubic inch Bugatti. If he could pull off the miracle of placing among the top finishers of the race the future of the stock model Cornelian would be secure. The Allegan factory would have to hire an extra shift to keep up with the flood of orders expected for the "speedy, easy riding light car, with the punch" that sold for $410.00 "top and windshield $25.00 extra."

The son of automotive pioneer Maurice E. Blood, young Blood had grown up amidst gasoline fumes, greasy knuckles and talk of four wheeled dreams. Like many another early automobile manufacturer, the elder Blood and his brother Clarence had cut their mechanical teeth on bicycles. They had established the Kalamazoo Cycle Co. on

North Rose Street in 1891. There they manufactured their popular "Fortune" brand bicycles and an innovative bicycle basket designed to carry doctor's medical bags as they made their rounds on "wheels."

By the gay 90's Kalamazoo had become one of the midwest's leading producers of horse drawn vehicles. Horseless carriages, then little more than rich men's toys, seemed to pose little threat to equine dominance. But the Bloods thought otherwise. Maurice Blood made quite a splash in the October 20, 1900, edition of the Kalamazoo *Telegraph* when he predicted that the automobile industry would become one of the country's largest and Kalamazoo might become as big an automobile center as it had for buggies.

The following year the Bloods opened Kalamazoo's first automobile dealership, handling the Mobile steam car. They made their initial sale in April, 1901, to Oscar K. Buckout, ironically, a prosperous manufacturer of embalming fluids.

Not content with merely selling other manufacturer's cars, by the following spring the Blood brothers had their own handmade prototype on the road. Resembling more a golf cart than a car, the 360 pound vehicle was powered by a tiny one cylinder air cooled engine. Thin wire spoked wheels clearly showed its bicycle heritage. Nevertheless, the Bloods logged more than 3,000 miles over Michigan's dusty roads that summer.

In October, 1902, the Bloods announced completion of an improved model that would sell for $400.00. That December they joined forces with another set of mechancial brothers from Kalamazoo, Frank and Charles Fuller, and formed the Michigan Automotive Co. The firm soon began marketing its Michigan two seater which weighed only 425 pounds and reputedly got 100 miles to the gallon.

After one year the Bloods withdrew from the

Beautiful Stream Line   *Fast as a Bullet*

Cornelian Light Car

$410 $410

Top and   Top and
Windshield   Windshield
$25 Extra $25 Extra

The Easiest Rider of Them All

Not a large car whittled down, but a **designed light car.** The following high-grade mechanical features are **built** into this little car:

Full floating rear axle.

Independent spring seat suspension. (Patented and a great feature.)

Stream line body with beautiful and durable baked enamel finish.

Fifteen large set New Departure ball bearings.

Standard tread. 100" wheelbase.

Thirty-one Chrome Vanadium steel special drop forgings

The most simple and the safest steering gear ever devised.

Sliding gear transmission with only three gears and no countershaft. (A real mechanical wonder.)

Sterling overhead valve motor; 2¾" x 4"; eighteen horsepower! a thousand pounds!

MECHANICALLY PERFECT

A speedy, easy riding light car, with the punch

BLOOD BROS. MACHINE COMPANY

ALLEGAN, MICHIGAN

Formerly of Kalamazoo

Less than 100 of the Cornelian cars were actually produced.

firm which eventually evolved into the Fuller Transmission Co.

By June, 1904, the new Blood Brothers Automobile and Machine Co. located on North Edwards Street had the prototype of a novel "side entrance tonneau touring car" on the road. A six passenger model weighing 1,700 pounds with a 16 horse-power engine, the new "Blood" sold for $1,500. Despite glowing reviews in automotive magazines, by 1906 the Blood had fallen victim to the intense competition that would eventually see over 2,500 distinct makes of cars produced in America. The renamed Blood Brother Machine Co. continued to produce its specialty - universal joints.

The next episode of the Blood automotive saga began following Howard Blood's graduation from the University of Michigan in 1909. Intrigued with articles about "cycle-cars" built in Europe and America, he determined to try his hand at constructing a very light car. In 1914 he built the first Cornelian in his father's barn.

The low to the ground, bathtub-shaped body of the vehicle was constructed of heavy sheet metal which made a channel frame unnecessary. Other revolutionary features included four wheel independent suspensions and a two speed trans axle which drove the rear wheels via U-jointed half-shafts. Light, smooth riding and fast despite its little 18 horse power engine, the Cornelian, as Blood later recalled, could "scoot around bigger cars that refused to give way on the grassy shoulder of the road.".

Blood's father and uncle took one look at the little gem and offered to commercially produce and market it. Their factory in Kalamazoo proved too small, however, and the Bloods began looking for a larger plant. Various cities in Michigan, Ohio and Iowa competed for the site of the new factory. But Mayor Burrell Tripp of Allegan clinched the plum for his community by promising to purchase and market 1,000 Cornelians. By late 1914, the Bloods had moved into the plant formerly occupied by the Allegan Mirror and Plate Glass Co.

Based on a successful showing against much larger cars in a Kalamazoo race in September 1914, Blood decided to enter the Cornelian in the Indianapolis 500 the following year. Chevrolet modified the engine and streamlined the body. All went well until during the 72nd lap of the two and a half mile course the Cornelian blew a valve and dropped out of the race. His dreams dashed, Blood sold the little race car then and there for use in dirt track racing and he never saw it again.

The Indianapolis debacle spelled defeat for the commercial production of Cornelians as well. Tripp's mammoth order evidently fell through and less than 100 Cornelians were actually manufactured before production was suspended in 1915. None appear to have survived. In retrospect, Blood realized his car was priced too low to make an adequate profit margin. He stated in 1966, "had I priced it at $500.00 it would have sold well and we could have made it a go."

Howard Blood left Allegan and eventually carved out a noted managerial career with Detroit Gear and Machine Company and Borg-Warner.

The Blood Brothers Company turned to sole production of universal joints, eventually becoming a subsidiary of the Rockwell-Standard Company, and remained Allegan's largest employer for many decades.

Joe Pete,
A Sugar Island Saga

Sugar Island, a 15 mile-long leg of land, thickly strewn with glacial boulders, lies in the St. Marys River just downstream from Sault Ste. Marie. Past its convoluted coast flow the waters of Lake Superior on their way to mingle with those of Lake Huron. Island resident know well the deep fog horn bellow of great freighters laden with wheat, taconite and coal.

Long the home of the native Ojibwa, the island draws its name from the maple trees that thrive there, a great sugar bush tapped by the Indians to produce countless birch bark mococks of pungent sugar. The Indian presence is still keenly felt and many prominent islanders proudly trace their Ojibwa lineage.

Sugar Island carries the distinction of being the last part of Michigan to have officially joined the state, its ownership contested by the British and not relinquished until 1842. Colorful place names dot its terrain, reminders of a fascinating heritage: Baie de Wassai, Church's Landing and Willwalk, an amalgam of village founder William Walker's name.

Still reached only via boat or the hourly passage of the Sugar Island Ferry, it has resisted development and remained a special place with a mystique all its own. Not surprisingly, several novelists such as Edwin Herbert Lewis, author of *White Lightning* (1923), have found set their works on the island. Poets also, including Michigan Governor Chase Osborn's wife Stellanova, have its rich heritage and picturesque geography irresistible. But it was the publication in 1929 of Florence McClinchey's *Joe Pete* that earned Sugar Island a secure niche on Michigan's literary map.

Set on the island in the decade before World War I, *Joe Pete* is a tragic story of the degradation of a beautiful young Ojibwa woman, symbolic in some respects of the fate of many Ojibwa people of that era. Stripped of their ancestral land, demoralized by the white man's whiskey and shunted aside to live in poverty they stubbornly clung to remnants of their native culture and their pride. The book is often not pleasant reading, nor should it be, but it truly captures the spirit of its theme and provokes the reader to better understand the native American's plight. In short, *Joe Pete* is a novel that should be required reading for all who cherish our state's heritage.

The novel opens with the birth of Joe Pete to his full-blooded Ojibwa parents, Mabel and Joe Shingoos. Her husband soon ships aboard a freighter and during his absence Mabel experiences a year of happiness, living on money sent by her husband and the sale to tourists of the ash baskets she fashions with traditional skill. This bright spot in her life ends with the return of her husband who grows jealous over the attention she lavishes on the baby. They quarrel and Joe deserts his family.

Mabel forms a liaison with a wandering Indian hunter, accompanies him to a logging camp and after he also deserts her is forced to rely on prostitution to feed herself and Joe Pete. As other children, half breeds, come, Mabel sinks lower and lower, becoming a drunkard, filthy, diseased, and she finally succumbs to an influenza epidemic that sweeps the island.

Meanwhile Joe Pete has emerged as a symbol of "all that is best in Indian character." He struggles against the misery and ugliness that surround him, hating the filth, the drunkenness and the brutal men who take advantage of his mother. Strong, able and kind, Joe Pete wins the affection and respect of all who know him. His people grow to recognize his strength of character and potential as a leader who can represent them in their struggle for better living conditions and equal rights.

A Sugar Island Indian pair believed to have been photographed by Florence McClinchey in the 1920s.

Other characters enliven the story line: old Nokomis, a grandmotherly herb woman; Big John, a wise and kind tribal leader; Jaakkola, a greedy, plotting Finlander; wealthy deer hunters from "down below" who have their way with Mabel; and there is a brief appearance by former Governor Osborn, who in real life lived on Duck Island, adjacent to Sugar Island. Florence McClinchey knew well of what she wrote. She later stated to a reviewer:

I became interested in the Sugar Island Indians because they have been my neighbors and friends for years. I really started out to get their tales and poems, but realized that their lives were splendid story material if I could tell it from the Indian viewpoint and as he would tell it, with economy of words. Everything in the books is true to actual happenings; though the incidents took place on more than one island in the St Marys River, and did not all happen to the one child, Joe Pete.

Born in Sault Ste. Marie in 1888, of English and Irish parentage, McClinchey was the only daughter in a family of nine children. She graduated from Sault High School, earned a teaching degree from the Michigan State Normal College at Ypsilanti. Returning to the Sault, she taught school there until the death of her parents. She then enrolled in the University of Michigan where she received her A.B. and M.A. degrees.

While attending college, McClinchey returned each summer to her beloved Sugar Island where she owned a log cabin at Baie de Wassai and continued to collect the material that she wove into the narrative of *Joe Pete*. She wrote her publishers, Henry Holt and Company:

My friends tell me that I am hard to get acquainted with and that I am too reserved. But I believe it was these two qualities which enabled me to become friends with the Indians and learn much of their legends and tales. I belong in the woods, and feel more natural there than in any other place. I am an expert in a canoe, and know how to manage a launch in a heavy sea. Those two accomplishments are ones about which I always boast.

In 1929 , the year *Joe Pete* was published, she joined the faculty of the English Department at Central Michigan University.

Joe Pete met with immediate success, receiving favorable reviews in *The New York Times, and The Saturday Review of Literature. The Boston Herald* called it "a first novel of undisputed excellence," The Book League of America, a forerunner to the Book of the Month Club, choose *Joe Pete* as its Christmas book selection. It went through five printings in November and December of 1929 alone. The volume remained popular throughout the 1930s, its distribution eventually being taken over by Grosset and Dunlap.

McClinchey continued her research on Sugar Island, collecting anecdotes, legends and local lore, but never published another book. She was working on a sequel to *Joe Pete* to be titled *Big John* when she died in 1946 as the result of an automobile accident while en route from Mount Pleasant to Sugar Island. Her masterpiece, *Joe Pete*, survives as a splendid account of Indian life on the island she loved so well.

Lake Michigan Lured
the Lincoln Scholar

On a September day in 1938 the staccato click and clack of an old manual typewriter filters down from the garret workshop of the big Dutch Colonial cottage nestled in the Lake Michigan sand dunes at Harbert. Thousands of books crowd the open shelves of rough lumber lining the four walls of the room. More books, pamphlets, files and manuscripts overflow boxes and bins and lie in great piles on tables and the floor.

Bent over the typewriter on a low worn table in the corner of the loft, a gaunt figure, white hair parted in the middle and streaming down almost over his eyes, punches out the type with big blunt working man's fingers:

"And the night came with great quiet
    And there was rest.
The prairie years, the war years, were over."

Carl Sandburg turned from the words he had written and taking off his thick glasses stood up to gaze at where the gray waters of the big lake flecked with an occasional white cap met the horizon.

It was done. He had completed the first draft of the work that had dominated his life over the succeeding ten years. There would come months more of revision as he honed and polished the 1,175,000 words of the book. But what any writer knows as the hardest task, the first draft, was over. In 1939 Harcourt Brace and Company would publish in four large volumes *Abraham Lincoln: The War Years.* The following year it would win Sandburg the Pulitzer Prize for history.

Illinois claims Sandburg as a native son because

he was born and raised there and his Chicago poems champion "the hog butcher to the world." North Carolina also lays claim to Sandburg because he spent his final years there. But Michigan, too, can count Sandburg among its literary immortals because he choose to live in Harbert from 1928-1945. And it was there that he wrote his magnum opus about Lincoln and the Civil War, an achievement that H.L. Menken called "the best American biography."

Born January 6, 1878, in Galesburg, Illinois, to Swedish immigrants August and Clara Sandburg, the man who would win fame as poet, newspaperman, biographer, children's author, ballad collector and folk singer, dropped out of school after the eight grade. Then came a succession of low paying jobs, hawking newspapers, delivering milk, shining shoes. In 1897 he hoboed boxcars to Iowa, Kansas, Nebraska and Colorado. Out west he worked building a railroad, as a farm hand, a "pearl driver" in a restaurant and in other pursuits which gave him a genuine understanding of working men.

When the Spanish American War broke out Sandburg enlisted in an Illinois infantry regiment and he served as a private in Puerto Rico. His military service brought him an appointment to West Point in 1899, but he failed the entrance examination in grammar and arithmetic. Later that year he entered Lombard College at Galesburg, supporting himself by working as a fireman and in the summer selling stereoscope cards door to door.

Wanderlust gripped him again in 1902 and he left college without graduating to wander the country selling stereoscope cards. Caught riding the rails near Pittsburgh, he spent ten days in the Allegheny County jail. The year 1904 found Sandburg back in his home town where he began writing a column in the Galesburg *Evening Mail*. Also that year his first poetry appeared in a slim booklet titled *In Reckless*

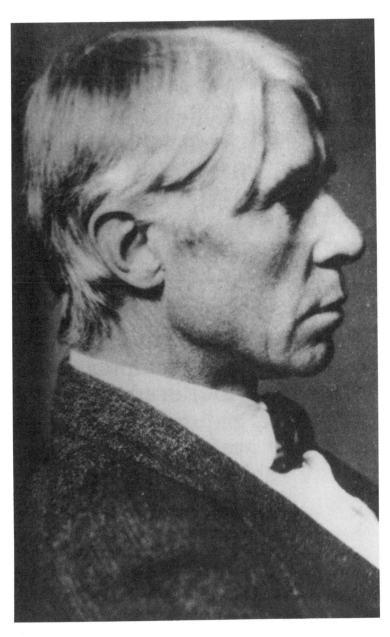

Carl Sandburg ca. 1935.

Ecstasy, privately published in an edition of 50 copies.

By 1907 Sandburg had become a Socialist. He worked as a district organizer for the Social Democratic party, gave Socialist speeches at Chautauquas, wrote a pamphlet published by the party and campaigned for Socialist presidential candidate Eugene V. Debs in 1908. In 1910 he served briefly as a private secretary to Emil Seidel, Socialist mayor of Milwaukee, and over the succeeding seven years he continued to write for Socialist journals and other Chicago periodicals. Through his work with the party he met another Socialist, Lilian Steichen, sister to photographer Edward Steichen, and in 1908 they married.

In 1912, Carl, Lilian and their baby, Margaret, moved to Chicago. Over the course of the following 16 years he would work for various Chicago newspapers and magazines and concentrate on his poetry. *Chicago Poems* (1916), *Corn-Huskers* (1918), *Smoke and Steel* (1920) and *Slabs of the Sunburnt West* brought national honors and a dedicated following but little financial reward.

That would change in 1926 with the publication of his two volume *Lincoln: The Prairie Years.* The *Pictorial Review* paid him $27,500 alone for serial rights for selected chapters of the work. Nevertheless Sandburg continued to work until 1932 for the *Chicago Daily News* at a salary of $75.00 a week.

By then the growing fame brought by this popular poetry, children's books and Lincoln biography had spurred the Sandburgs to move from their Elmhurst, Illinois, home to a site less accessible to admirers, the Harbert sand dunes..

When Sandburg first fell under Michigan's spell is open to conjecture. As early as 1907 he delivered Lyceum lectures on Walt Whitman to audiences at Buckley and two other Michigan locations. Sometime prior to 1920 an acquaintance with Kalamazoo had inspired him to pen a poem on its "sins." In the 1920s the Sandburg family, like many other Chicago area resorters, discovered Michigan's lakeside sand dunes to be a mecca for summertime fun. The summer of 1927 found them vacationing near Three Oaks. That year also Sandburg invested some of the proceeds from his first Lincoln books in a five acre tract of sand dunes at Harbert.

The following May the family moved into the large cottage designed by Lilian they built there. A chicken house, two barns and a milk house completed the country estate the Sandburgs named "Chickaming" after its original Indian residents. The outbuildings allowed Lilian to further develop the specialty she became one of the nation's leading authorities on - the breeding of pedigreed dairy goats.

The broad sand beach offered much needed relaxation for the overworked Sandburg. He walked the beach gathering driftwood and sometimes practiced his golf drive. There, too, the three Sandburg daughters, Margaret, Janet and Helga, grew to womanhood. In the 1960s Helga would use Harbert as a setting for *Blueberry* and some of her other novels.

His daughters and Lilian also assisted Sandburg in the tremendous undertaking of bringing order to the massive collection of Lincoln material he collected at the cottage. He acquired bound volumes of the *Congressional Globe* for the Civil War years, the 133 volume *Official Records of the Rebellion*, more than 4,000 books and pamphlets on Lincoln as well as file after file of manuscript sources and oral history recollections. To make space in the garret for the collection Sandburg ripped pertinent pages from some bindings and stored the mutilated volumes in a barn - not a practice recommended by this book lover.

Through his passionate study Sandburg became the world's leading authority on Lincoln. In his writing he sought to take Lincoln off the lofty pedestal where he had been placed by previous biographers and reveal, in the words of Karl Detzer who interviewed Sandburg at Harbert in 1941:

A human Lincoln with his share of human fragilities, a Lincoln guarded by ambition, devotion, dislike, mistrust, stubbornness - by all the complex and warring elements that make up any human being - as well as by a deep humility and sympathy for all human struggles.

Sandburg began work on *The War Years* in earnest in October, 1928. Six months later he optimistically estimated that he would require another five or six years to finish the project. It actually took nearly twice that long. Sandburg was fifty when he started writing *The War Years*, an age he thought appropriate. He later admitted "Between forty and fifty I would have had more drive but less perspective, less understanding, less wisdom, and less experience. But had I waited until I was sixty, I would not have had the physical endurance to finish the job."

Despite his preoccupation with the Lincoln book Sandburg found time to help manage the goat farm, publish at least eight other books of poetry and juvenile stories, travel to frequent lecture appearances and maintain ample correspondence. The letters to and from his friends that flowed into the tiny Harbert post office comprise a roster of some of America's leading literary lights: H.L. Menken, Sherwood Anderson, Helen Keller, Ezra Pound, Ole Rolvaag, William Rose Benet, Archibald MacLeish, Christopher Morley, Allan Nevins and Douglas Southall Freeman.

In 1945 President Harry S. Truman wrote Sandburg about his Lincoln books saying "not in my day will there be produced another study of the great Civil War President which will supersede them." Sandburg responded: "Your deeply moving letter about those Lincoln volumes has been framed and put on a wall in our house because near twenty years in the house was given to those books and your words are a sort of attention that the work has a living use."

But before the year was over the Sandburgs moved from Harbert to a 235 acre farm near Flat Rock, North Carolina, ironically once the summer home of C. G. Memminger, Jefferson Davis' Secretary of the Treasury. Concern for Lilian's health, the desire for a large farm with pasture for the goats and the availability of the Memminger place at a bargain price inspired the move.

Sandburg continued his literary career in North Carolina. On his 85th birthday he published his final book *Honey and Salt*. He died July 22, 1967.

Renovated in the 1980s, Sandburg's Harbert home has been featured in local architectual tours. And the Lincoln books he wrote there, Michigan classics measured by any yardstick, are, according to Pulitzer prize winning dramatist and historian Robert E. Sherwood, "a monument that will stand forever - a monument to subject and author alike."

New Books For Old

Roccoco bindings, marbled boards and burnished gold edges cascaded down its sides as the mountain of books grew higher by the minute. The dog-eared pages of pioneer primers, household guides and huge family bibles carefully carried in covered wagons to Michigan Territory fluttered in the breeze. Archaic law tomes in tan calf bindings, arcane divinity tracts, saccharine Victorian novels, poetry penned and published by bucolic bards and great-grandmothers' well thumbed cook books mingled in a great heap of bygone literature. What rare bibliographic treasures lay buried within the dross will never be known.

Never before had a library of such magnitude been collected in southwest Michigan. Never had Michigan seen such an assemblage of book minded people. Some 5,000 strong, they thronged the Allegan County Fairgrounds on May 7, 1940, to celebrate the successful outcome of the "New-for-Old-Book" campaign.

The promise of "new books for old" at a rate of five old for one new had spurred a frenzied ransacking of dusty attics, ancient immigrant trunks and front parlor shelves for little read volumes. The W.K. Kellogg Foundation had launched the campaign "expecting to have to provide a few hundred new books." But school children throughout the seven rural counties included in the program had feverishly lugged in packing cases, paper bags and gunny sacks full of old books. Allegan County outdid itself in its bibliophilic efforts. From Allegan flowed 22,678 volumes, Plainwell 28,545, Wayland 10,216, Otsego 29,776, and so it went throughout Allegan County until an amazing total of 180,399 old books had been collected.

Battle Creek cereal czar, William Keith Kellogg,

had established the foundation which took his name in 1930 to continue his philanthropic activities in the "the promotion of the health, education, and welfare of mankind, but principally of children and youth, directly or indirectly." Early on the foundation had adopted a policy to "use its resources mainly in the application of knowledge rather than in research or relief."

The Kellogg Foundation's initial target area became the rural counties surrounding Battle Creek. It identified within that area a situation common to thousands of other rural communities throughout the United States, namely "health programs were practically non-existence, many schools were neglected and inadequate, and community facilities, such as hospitals and libraries, were often either absent or of poor quality."

The Kellogg Foundation determined to provide funds for cooperative community programs of a social character in an effort to stimulate communities to help themselves. The first step was to promote the creation of county health departments, heretofore absent in all of the seven counties. By 1941, all of those counties had in place health departments with the foundation contributing 65% of their budgets. Other areas in which the foundation focused its resources included consolidation of rural schools, hot lunch and milk programs, school hygiene, improved dental services, creation and upgrading of hospital and health centers, summer camps, special education, etc.

The program "to place local libraries on a par with other agencies which make for a healthy and sound community life" began with the creation of a library at the foundation headquarters in Battle Creek. It circulated books throughout the seven counties much like the current interlibrary loan program. Next came a public awareness campaign with the theme: "All that mankind has done, thought, gained or been,

A familiar scene in hundreds of southwest Michigan schoolhouses during the 1940 "New Books for Old" campaign.

is lying as in magic preservation in the pages of books."

But the foundation encountered widespread reluctance by rural library trustees to invest funds in books because "they were not read anyhow." Analysis of library holdings pointed to an over supply of older books and few modern, more attractive publications. In an effort to upgrade collections, the foundation launched a highly promoted six-week drive in 1940, promising village and rural school libraries one new book for every five old books turned in.

Much to the foundation's surprise, the entire campaign held within the counties of Allegan, Barry, Eaton, Van Buren, Hillsdale, Branch and Calhoun yielded 900,000 old books! Next came a series of "book fairs" where consultants helped librarians choose new volumes from lists of approved books. Thousands of Allegan County residents, for example, attended the book fair held at Allegan's Griswold Auditorium on September 30 through October 4, 1940. By 1942 the Kellogg Foundation had expended $436,655 for library purposes at a time when new hardbound books sold for $3.00 or less.

The resulting "renaissance in southwestern Michigan libraries" also created a demand for better trained librarians. The foundation made a grant to what was then Western Michigan College for the creation of a Department of Librarianship. Beginning in 1948 WMC trained librarians brought increased professionalism to rural libraries throughout the state.

Sadly, from the point of view of many lovers of old books, the 900,000 volumes collected at the Allegan County Fairgrounds and other sites throughout the seven counties were loaded on semi-trucks, hauled to area paper mills and pulped up. The 180,000 new books which replaced them were labeled with a special bookplate documenting their source.

While ultimately those books too outlasted their usefulness and most have in turn been discarded, the healthy condition of many libraries throughout southwestern Michigan bears witness to the success of the Kellogg Foundation's stimulus more than five decades ago.

Nevertheless, it is a bitter-sweet experience to purchase discarded volumes at many a southwestern Michigan library sale, as I have, bearing the bookplate "Library Day - Five for One - One for All - Education - Cooperation - Recreation.'

As the Fate of a River
So Goes Ours

Like the river of time, the great Kalamazoo meanders through Jackson, Calhoun, Kalamazoo and Allegan counties' past, present and future. For the Potawatomi and Ottawa it was the Ke-Kalamazoo, "the place of boiling water," probably in reference to its rock strewn rapids. For the bands of Indians who wintered along its banks it was their highway and their sustenance. In birch bark canoes they harvested the wild rice that thrived at the shallows near its mouth. They collected also the berries, nuts, roots, huge egg shaped puffballs and medicinal plants which grow along its banks and adjoining lowlands.

From its pure waters they netted trout, bass and pickerel. They watched from atop high sandy bluffs for enormous sturgeon making their way up the shallows, then ran down to wrestle the prehistoric-looking monsters to shore.

With flint tipped arrows they stalked the whitetails who came to lap its waters. They garnered from the immense flocks of passenger pigeons that bent trees low over it banks. Rabbits, squirrels, woodchucks and great snapping turtles that lumbered from the swamps in the spring to lay their eggs in the sun-warmed sand filled their cooking pots. They trapped muskrats, otters, fishers, mink, and martin for their furs. They shared the land's largesse with black bears, panthers, wildcats, wolves and eagles. There was more than enough for all.

For the white pioneers who streamed into the Kalamazoo River Valley in the 1830s the river also served as thoroughfare. From Kalamazoo entrepreneurs floated great arks loaded with flour and other foodstuffs to the port villages at the river's mouth. From there, wind blown crafts wafted those staples to hungry cities.

The arrival of the Michigan Central Railroad that snaked west to link with civilization Jackson in 1841, Battle Creek in 1845 and Kalamazoo a year later ended that era. But for the settlements that dotted its banks below, the river long retained its importance as a shipping route. River steamers, scores of which took shape in shipyards along its banks, continued to ply the length of the Kalamazoo from Allegan to its mouth until 1868 when the first railroad locomotive that chugged into the city at the big ox bows also ended that shipping monopoly.

But it was the vast stands of white pine, which blanketed the terrain north and west of Allegan that ushered in the colorful era of the shanty boy and the river hog, the double-bitted ax and the peavy, the rollway and the wanigan, a chuck wagon type craft that followed the log drive. In 1834, Oka Town and Abijah Chichester floated the first rafts of lumber from Pine Creek (a ghost town just west of Otsego) to Newark (now Saugatuck). During the following four decades as lumber barons lustily converted the pine forest to cemetery-like stretches of stumps the waters of the Kalamazoo heaved with great glistening pine logs. Old timer's fondly remembered the days when they could jump across log to log from one bank of the river to another without getting their feet wet.

Sawmills at Allegan, Dunningville, Swan Creek and Singapore, now buried beneath sand dunes, and elsewhere buzzed through millions of feet of lumber. Unfortunately, the mountains of sawdust casually pushed into the current began to poison the river, choking its channel and ruining untold spawning grounds.

Beginning also in the pioneer era and continuing well into the 20th century every single settlement through which the Kalamazoo flowed would callously dump its effluvia into the waters, out

STEAMER MILDRED, ALLEGAN, MICH.

The steamer *Mildred* once carried happy recreationists along the bright Kalamazoo.

of sight and out of mind, except to the communities downstream. Urban areas like Kalamazoo and Battle Creek created grandiose sewer systems whose terminuses were simply the Kalamazoo River. By the 1880s streams that fed waste into the river, such as Arcadia Creek in downtown Kalamazoo, had become so noisome that they were buried in culverts. But still they continued to spew into the Kalamazoo

Worse yet, came the paper mills. The granddaddy of them all, the Kalamazoo Paper Company, located on Portage Creek, a tributary of the Kalamazoo River, in 1867. It served as a nesting ground for a meager flock of young paper makers who began planting there own mills along the Kalamazoo River. By the turn of the century Otsego had two big mills, Plainwell another and soon Kalamazoo's dozen mills would win it title as "the world's largest producer of paper."

Those paper mills did not locate on the Kalamazoo River because of the scenic vistas afforded employees. Paper making requires a great supply of water and it produces equally huge quantities of pollutants, most easily gotten rid of by flushing them into the stream. The Kalamazoo River became little more than an open sewer.

Nor were the paper mills the sole culprits. Blatantly or surrepitiously, practically every other industry located near the river sent its noxious wastes downstream. The various pollutants took their toll, not all at once but gradually, as any slowly induced poison would. Turn-of-the-century steamboats like the *Mildred,* which once carried gaily dressed excursionists on river outings, stopped running because the river stank so.

The cities through which the river flowed turned their backs on the Kalamazoo - it was no longer an asset but an embarrassment. In 1953, *Life Magazine* focused the nation's attention on the river's plight through an illustration of "four acres of dead carp on the Kalamazoo," suffocated because the flowing water held no oxygen whatsoever.

In recent years, efforts by the E.P.A. and environmental activists have succeeded in enhancing the appearance and smell, at least, of the Kalamazoo. But what poisons yet lurk in its muddy bottom is best left to the imagination.

The fate of the river cotinues to be inextricably linked to the succeeding generations who look to it for recreation, employment and solace.

Yes, anglers continue to plumb its murky waters, in quest of coho salmon and other fish not native to its slow currents. And those who consume their catch over any length of time can often be distinguished by their slurred speech and facial tics.

Maybe some day the Kalamazoo will return to its former glory, an asset that can be touched and tasted as well as looked at. For now, those who have grown up on and love the river despite its problems, get a perverse chuckle out of watching vacationers from Chicago water skiing, swimming and frolicing in the muddy bottom of Lake Allegan, a dammed up section of the Kalamazoo River.

SOURCES

Hennepin & the Griffin

Dunbar, Willis F. & May, George S. *Michigan: A History of the Wolverine State*. Grand Rapids, [1980].

Greenly, Albert Harry. *A Selective Bibliography of ...Michigan History*. Lunenburg, Vermont, 1958.

Howes, Wright. *U.S. Iana*. New York, 1962.

Marshall, O.H. "The Building and Voyage of the Griffon in 1679," *Publications of the Buffalo Historical Society*. Vol. 1 (1879) p. 253.

Quaife, Milo. *Lake Michigan*. Indianapolis, [1944].

Shea, John Gilmary, ed. *A Description of Louisiana by Father Louis Hennepin*. New York, 1880.

Thwaites, Reuben Gold, ed. *A New Discovery of a Vast Country in America by Father Louis Hennepin*. 2 Vols. Chicago, 1903.

Judgement at Mackinac

Bayliss, Joseph E. & Estelle and Quaife, Milo. *River of Destiny: The Saint Marys*. Detroit, 1955.

"Capital Punishment in Michigan, 1683: Duluth at Michilimackinac," *Michigan History*. Vol. 50, No. 4. (December 1966) p. 349.

"Indian Murdererrs Punished By DuLuth," *Wisconsin Historical Collection*. Vol. XVI [1902] p. 114.

Kellogg, Louise Phelps. *Early Narratives of the Northwest*. New York, [1917].

McLennan, William. "A Gentleman of the Royal Guard." *Harper's New Monthly Magazine*. Vol. LXXXVII, No. DXX. [Sept.1893]. p. 609.

Neill, Edward D. *History of the Ojibways and Their Connection With Fur Traders*. Reprint Edtion. Minneapolis, 1970.

Sheldon, Electa M. *The Early History of Michigan...* New York, 1856.

Story, Norah. *The Oxford Companion to Canadian History and Literature*. Toronto, 1967.

Robert Rogers

Greenly: *Bibliography of Michigan History*.

Peckham, Howard H. *Pontiac and the Indian Uprising*. Princeton, 1947.

Rogers, Robert. *A Concise Account of North America...*

London, 1765.

_____. *Journals of...* Albany, 1883.

_____. *Ponteach or the Savages of America with an introduction and a biography of the author by Allan Nevins.* Chicago, 1914.

Joseph Bates - Hell on the High Seas

Massie, Larry B. and Schmitt, Peter J. *Battle Creek: The Place Behind the Product.* Woodland Hills, California, [1984].

Tucker, Glenn. *Poltroons and Patriots: A Popular Account of the War of 1812.* 2 Vols. Indianapolis, [1954].

White, James, ed. *The Early Life and Later Experiences and Labors of Elder Joseph Bates.* Battle Creek, 1878.

Leonard Slater

Gordon, Douglas H. & May, George S. "Michigan Journal, 1836, John M. Gordon," *Michigan History.* Vol. 43, No. 4. (Dec. 1959) p. 433.

Hayne, Coe. *Baptist Trial - Makers of Michigan.* Philadelphia, 1936.

History of Allegan & Barry Counties, Michigan. Phila.delphia, 1880.

Little, Henry. "Grand Rapids History," *Michigan Pioneer Collections.* Vol. 4. (1884). p. 286.

Lydens, Z.Z., ed. *The Story of Grand Rapids.* Grand Rapids, 1966.

McCoy, Isaac. *History of Baptist Indian Missions.* Washington, 1840.

Potter, W.W. *History of Barry County.* [Grand Rapids, 1912].

St. John, Mrs. W.E. "Daily Life, Manners, and Customs of the Indians in Kalamazoo County," *Michigan Pioneer Collections.* Vol. 10 [1886] p. 166.

Van Buren, A.D.P. "Indian Reminiscences of Calhoun and Kalamazoo Counties, *"Michigan Pioneer Collections.* Vol. 10 (1888) p. 147.

Bark Covered House

Greenly: *Bibliography of Michigan History.*

Nowlin, William. *The Bark Covered House, or Back in the Woods Again...* Detroit, 1876 [Lakeside Press reprint edited by Milo Quaife. Chicago, 1937].

Klutzes on the Frontier

Armstrong, Joe and Pahl, John. *River & Lake: A*

263

Sesquicentenial History of Allegan County, Michigan.
N.P., [1985].
History of Allegan and Barry Counties, Michigan.
Thomas, Henry F. *Twentieth Century History of Allegan County.* Chicago, 1907.

Pictured Rocks Tourists
Carter, James L. *Voyageurs' Harbor: A History of the Grand Maris Country.* Marquette, 1977.
"Gilman, Chandler R.," *The American Annual Cyclopedia and Register of Important Events of the Year 1865.* N.Y., 1868. p. 402.
[Gilman, Chandler R.] *Life on the Lakes...* 2 Vols. New York, 1836.
Hubach, Robert R. *Early Midwestern Travel Narratives: An Annotated Bibliography 1634-1850.* Detroit, 1961.
Wilson, James Grant and Fiske, John, eds. *Appleton's Cyclopedia of American Biography.* 6 Vols. New York, 1888.
Wood, Edwin O. *Historic Mackinac...* 2 Vols. New York, 1918.

Yankee Lewis
"Actual Site of Yankee Bill's Famous Hostelry, *"Hastings Banner,* 1 May 1958.
History of Allegan & Barry County, Michigan.
Potter: *History of Barry County.*
White, George H. "Yankee Lewis' Famous Hostelry In the Wilderness," *Michigan Pioneer Collections* Vol. 26 (1894-1895) p. 302.

Wolves
Allen, Durward L. *Wolves of Minong.* Boston, 1979.
Burt, William H. *The Mammals of Michigan.* Ann Arbor, 1946.
Caesar, Gene. *The Wild Hunters.* New York, [1957].
History of Berrien and Van Buren Counties... Philadelphia, 1880.
Mech, L. David. *The Wolves of Isle Royale.* Washington, 1966.
Michigan Biographies. 2 vols. Lansing, 1924.
Rowland, O.W. *A History of Van Buren County...* 2 vols. Chicago, 1912.

Anna Jameson
Jameson, Anna B. *Winter Studies and Summer Rambles.* 3 Vols. London, 1838.

Kunitz, Stanley J. and Haycraft Howard, eds. *British Authors of the Nineteenth Century*. New York, 1936.
Martineau, Harriet. *Society in America*. 3 Vols. London, 1837.
Story: *Canadian History and Literature*.
Wood: *Historic Mackinac*.

Dr. William Upjohn
Carlisle, Robert D.B. *A Century of Caring: The Upjohn Story*. [Elmsford, N.Y., 1987].
Engel, Leonard. *Medicine Makers of Kalamazoo*. New York, [1961].
History of Allegan and Barry Counties, Michigan.
Potter: *Barry County*.
Record of Service of Michigan Volunteers in the Civil War. Seventh Michigan Cavalry. [Kalamazoo, 1903].
Redpath, Frederich Lawrence. *A String in the Fabric: The Story of the Upjohn Family*. Senior Thesis, Department of History, Princeton University. April, 1939.
Walton, Esther. "Some History of the Upjohn House," *Hastings Banner*. May 14, 1987.

Cass Crosses the Sea
[Cass, Lewis]. *France, Its King, Court, and Government*. New York, 1840.
Field, Maunsell B. *Memories of Many Men and of Some Women...* New York, 1874.
McLaughlin, Andrew C. *Lewis Cass*. Boston, [1919].
Michigan Biographies.
Smith, W.L.G. *The Life and Times of Lewis Cass*. New York, 1856.
Woodford, Frank B.. *Lewis Cass the Last Jeffersonian*. New Brunswick, 1950.

Six Months in the Allegan Forest
Cook, Darius B. *Six Months Among Indians...* Niles, 1889, (reprint Berrien Springs, 1974).
History of Berrien and Van Buren Counties.
Van Buren, Anson, D.P. "Noonday the Ottawa Chief..." *Michigan Pioneer Collections*. Vol. 10 (1886) p. 158.

Wilson E. Edsell & Olivet College
Dunbar, Willis F. *The Michigan Record in Higher Education*. Detroit, 1963.
Durant, Samuel M. *History of Ingham and Eaton Counties*,

Michigan. Philadelphia, 1880.
History of Allegan and Barry Counties.
Michigan Biographies.
The Ohio Guide. N.Y., [1940].
Williams, Wolcott B. *A History of Olivet College.* Olivet, 1901.

Pitezel in the Upper Peninsula

Macmillan, Margaret Burnham. *The Methodist Church in Michigan: The Nineteenth Century.* Grand Rapids, [1967].
Pitezel, John H. *The Backwoods Boy Who Became a Minister...* New York, [1859].
_____. *Lights and Shades of Missionary Life...* Cincinnati, 1857.
_____. *Stray Leaves From the Budget of an Itinerant.* Cincinnati, 1861.
Reuter, Dorothy and Brunger, Ronald A. *Methodist Indian Ministries in Michigan, 1830-1990.* Grand Rapids, [1993].
Rezek, Antoine Ivan. *History of the Diocese of Sault Ste. Marie and Marquette...* 2 Vols. Houghton, 1907.
Verwyst, P. Chryostomus. *Life and Labors of Rt. Rev. Frederic Baraga...* Milwaukee, 1900.
Walling, Regis M. and Rupp, N. Daniel, eds. *The Diary of Bishop Frederic Baraga.* Detroit, 1990.

The Junction

Baxter, Albert. *History of the City of Grand Rapids, Michigan.* New York, 1891.
The First Hundred Years. Plainwell 1869-1969. N.P., [1969].
History of Allegan and Barry Counties.
Mason, Philip P. "The Plank Road Craze: A Chapter in the History of Michigan's Highways," *Great Lakes Informant.* Series 2 No. 1.
Stoddard, Asa H. *Miscellaneous Poems.* Kalamazoo, 1880.
Whitney, Joan. *History of Plainwell, Michigan.* Dallas, Texas, 1978.

H.H. Riley & Puddleford Papers

American Biographical History of Emminent and Self-Made Men... Michigan Volume. Cincinnati, 1878. (Fourth Congressional District. p. 55.
Cutler, Harry G. *History of St. Joseph, Michigan.* 2 Vols. Chicago, 1911.
Michigan Biographies.

Michigan Pioneer Collections. 40 Vols. 1874-1929.

Riley, Henry H. *The Puddleford Papers; or Humors of the West.* Boston, 1875.

Silliman, Sue I. "Paper Villages of St. Joseph County," *Michigan History Magazine.* Vol. 4. Nos. 2-3. [April-July, 1920]. p. 588.

Village of Constantine Sesquicentennial 1828-1978.

Oxen

Adams, John J. "Early History of Lenawee County," *Michigan Pioneer Collections.* Vol. 2 (1877-78) p. 357.

Census and Statistics of the State of Michigan May 1854. Lansing, 1854.

History of Allegan & Barry Counties.

Howell, Andrew. Address at Annual Reunion of the Lenewee County Pioneer Society," *Michigan Pioneer Collections.* Vol. 13. [1888]. p. 586.

Michigan State Agricultural Society Report. Lansing, 1855.

"The Yoke-Makers of Michigan." compiled by W.P.A. N.P., N.D.

Grandma Moulton

Moulton, Mary C. *True Stories of Pioneer Life.* Detroit, 1924.

Robertson, John. *Michigan in the War.* Lansing, 1882.

The Otsego Vision

Carson, Gerald. *Cornflake Crusade.* New York, [1957].

Loughborough, J.N. *The Great Second Advent Movement its Rise and Progress.* Nashville, Tenn. [1905].

Massie and Schmitt: *Battle Creek.*

Noorbergen, Rene. *Ellen G. White: Prophet of Destiny.* New Canaan, Conn., [1972].

Schwarz, Richard W. *John Harvey Kellogg, M.D.* Nashville, Tenn. [1970].

Stoltz, Duff. Telephone interview. 5 July 1989.

C.B. Lewis' Quad's Odds

Beal, W.J. *History of the Michigan State Agricultural College...* East Lansing, 1915.

Goodrich, Madge K. *A Bibliography of Michigan Authors.* Richmond, Va., 1928.

Harrison, Dale "Two Anniversaries This Week of Note in Michigan," *Kalamazoo Gazette* (?). 16 Feb. 1936.

Holden, Edward G. "Little Journeys in Journalism,"

Michigan History Magazine. Vol. XI, No. 40. (July, 1927). p. 424.
Kirke, Edmund "The City of the Strait," *Harper's New Monthly Magazine.* Vol. 73, No. 435 (August, 1886) p. 327.
Lewis, Charles B. *Quad's Odds...*Detroit, 1875.
Marquis, Albert Nelson. *Who's Who in America* Vol. 6, 1911.
Rowell, George P. & Co. *American Newspaper Directory.* New York, 1869.
Sanford, George P. "Reminiscential," *Michigan Pioneer Collections.* Vol. 6 (1884). p. 292.

C.W. Jay in Oceana County

Hartwick, L.M. and Tuller, W.H. *Oceana County Pioneers and Business Men of Today..* Pentwater, 1890.
History of Oceana County, Michigan... Chicago, 1882.
Jay, Charles W. *My New Home in Northern Michigan, and Other Tales.* Trenton, N.J., 1874.
Oceana County, Michigan, Topography, Biography, History, Art Folio... Battle Creek, 1895.
Romig, Walter. *Michigan Place Names.* Detroit, 1986.

A.H. Stoddard, The Farmer Poet

[Durant, Samuel.] *History of Kalamazoo County.* Philadelphia, 1880.
Christlieb, Ward: Interview. 17 October 1989.
Stoddard, A.H. "Biographical Sketches" (Unpublished manuscript written in 1893 and 1900).
Stoddard, A.H. *Miscellaneous Poems.* Kalamazoo, 1880.

Glory Days of Grayling

Barnett, LeRoy. *Railroads in Michigan: A Catalog of Company Publication, 1836-1980.* Marquette, 1986.
Drews, Robin A. ed. "The Michigan Grayling: 1880 Essay and Letters of Martin Metcalf," *Michigan History.* Vol. 45. No. 2 (June 1961) p. 135.
Goode, G. Brown. *American Fishes...* New York, 1888.
A Guide to the Health, Pleasure, Game and Fishing Resorts of Northern Michigan Reached by the Grand Rapids and Indiana Railroad. Chicago, 1881.
Hubbs, Carl L and Lagler, Karl F. *Fishes of the Great Lakes Region.* Ann Arbor, [1958].
Manual for the Use of the Legislature of Michigan. Lansing, 1873-1879.
Mershon, William B. *Recollections of My Fifty Years Hunting*

and Fishing. Boston, 1923.

Miller, Hazen L. *The Old Au Sable.* Grand Rapids. [1964].

Norris, Thaddeus. "The Michigan Grayling," *Scribner's Monthly.* Vol. XIX (November, 1879) p. 17.

Northrup, A. Judd. *Camps and Tramps in the Adirondocks and Grayling Fishing in Northern Michigan...* Syracuse, N.Y., 1880.

Petersen, Eugene T. "Vacation in Northern Michigan, 1879," *Michigan History.* Vol. 42. No. 2 (June, 1958). p. 154.

Powers, Perry F. *A History of Northern Michigan.* 3 Vols. Chicago. 1912.

Littlejohn's Legends

Armstrong & Pahl:. *River & Lake.*

History of Oceana County, Michigan.

Littlejohn, Flavius J. *Legends of Michigan and the Old North West.* Allegan, 1875.

Reid, E.C. "Death of the Venerable Judge Littlejohn." *Michigan Pioneer Collections.* Vol. 3, (1881). p. 310.

Van Buren, A.D.P. "Sketches, Reminiscences, and Anedotes of the Old Member of the Calhoun and Kalamazoo County Bars," *Michigan Pioneer Collections.* Vol. XI. (1887), p. 271.

Charles Blakemen - Shanty Boy

Blakeman, Charles E. *Report of a Truant: A True Story.* [Grand Rapids, 1928].

Holbrook, Stewart. *Holy Old Mackinaw...* New York, 1938.

Titus, C.O. *Atlas of Allegan County, Michigan.* Philadelphia, 1873.

Allegan Man-Eater

History of Allegan and Barry Counties, Michigan...

Magner, Dennis. *The Art of Taming and Educatiing the Horse...* Battle Creek, 1884.

_____. *The Farmer's Encyclopedia...* Akron, Ohio, 1901.

_____. *The New System of Educating Horses...* 10th ed., revised. Buffalo, 1874.

Pahl, John: Telephone interview. 11 July 1995.

Record of Service of Michigan Volunteers in the Civil War. Fourteenth Michigan Infantry. [Kalamazoo, 1903].

_____   _____.

Ninetenth Michigan Infantry. [Kalamazoo, 1903].

Thomas. *Twentieth Century History of Allegan County.*

The Battle of Manton

Cadillac Evening News. Centennial History Sections. June 12-July 17, 1971.
Disbrow, Willard: Interview at Manton Musum. 7 July 1995.
Manton Area Then and Now. N.P. [1985].
The Manton Tribune. 11 April 1882.
Peterson , William R. *The View From Courthouse Hill.* Philadelphia, [1972].
Powers: *History of Northern Michigan.*

George E. Bardeen, Paper Magnate

Across the Web. Bicentennial Issue of Mead Paperboard Products. Newsletter. Otsego, 1976.
Illustrated Atlas of Allegan County, Michigan. Racine, Wis., 1895.
Kalamazoo City Directory, 1891. Kalamazoo, 1891.
Massie, Larry B. and Schmitt, Peter J. *Kalamazoo: The Place Behind the Products.* Woodland Hills, Cal. 1981.
Meyers, R. "'History of Otsego paper Mills,'' Unpublished Typescript of Talk Presented at Allegan County Historical Society. 19 Nov. 1958.
Michigan Bureau of Labor and Industrial Statistics. 10th Annual Report. Lansing, 1903.
Paper Manufacturers of the Kalamazoo Valley. N.P. [1915].
Rowe, Ford F. *Kalamazoo The Debt-Free City.* N.P. [1939].
Weissert, Charles A. *An Account of Kalamazoo County.* Vol. 3 of *Historic Michigan Land of the Great Lakes. George N. Fuller, ed.* N.P., [1927].

Mackinac Island Souvenirs

Greenwood, John Orville. *Namesakes 1930-1955.* Cleveland, [1978].
Petersen, Eugene T. *Mackinac Island: Its History in Pictures.* Mackinac Island, 1973.
Polk's Gazetter of Michigan. Detroit. 1890-1915.
Stenfano, Frank, Jr. *Pictorial Souvenirs & Commemoratives of North America.* New York, 1976.

W.R. Shafter, Galesburg Hero

Alger, Russel A. *The Spanish American War.* New York, 1901.
Anderson, William M. *They Died to Make Men Free: A History of the 19th Michigan Infantry in the Civil War.* Berrien Springs, MI. 1980.

Bonsal, Stephen. *The Fight for Santiago.* New York, 1899.
Brownlee, James Henry, ed. *Wartime Echoes.* Akron, [1898].
Carlton, S.H. "Reminiscences of Gen. Shafter," *Michigan History Magazine.* Vol. X. No. 35 [April 1926] p. 265.
Davis, Richard Harding. *The Cuban and Porto Rican Campaigns.* New York, 1898
Dunbar, Willis F. *Kalamazoo and How It Grew.* Kalamazoo, 1959.
Durant,: *History of Kalamazoo County,*
Fitzgibbon, John. "Michigan in the Spanish American War," *Michigan History Magazine.* Vol. XII, No. 1 [Jan. 1928] p. 77.
Freidel, Frank. *The Splendid Little War.* Boston, [1958].
Galesburg Area Centennial 1869-1969. Kal-Gal Printing Co. [1969].
Millis, Walter. *The Martial Spirit...* Boston, 1931.
Reid, Jasper B. Jr. "Russell A. Alger as Secretary of War," *Michigan HIstory Magazine.* Vol. 43. No. 2 [June 1959]. p. 225.
Rhodes, Charles D. "William Rufus Shafter," *Michigan History Magazine.* Vol. XVI [Autumn 1932] p. 371.
Robertson,: *Michigan in the War.*
Shafter, William R. "The Capture of Santiago De Cuba," *Century Magazine.* Vol. LVII, No. 4, [Feb. 1899]. p. 612.
Wheeler, Joseph. *The Santiago Campaign 1898.* Boston, 1898.

A.M. Todd's Big Barn

Armstrong and Pahl: *River and Lake.*
Landing, James E. *American Essence.* Kalamazoo [1969].
Lane, Kit, ed. *The History of Western Allegan County.* [Dallas, Texas, 1988].
Massie and Schmitt: *Kalamazoo.*
Todd, Albert M. "The Essential Oil Industry of Michigan," *Thirty-ninth Annual Report of Secretary of the State Board of Agriculture.* [1900], p. 400.

Hiawatha at Petoskey

The Indian Play Hiawatha at Wa-Ya-Ga-Mug... [Grand Rapids, 1906].
Jarvis, Nancy H. ed. *Historical Glimpses Petoskey.* Petoskey, 1986.

Kunitz, Stanley J. and Haycraft, Howard. *American Authors 1600-1900.* New York, 1938.
Longfellow, Henry Wadsworth. *The Song of Hiawatha.* "The Players Edition." Chicago, [1911].
Mason, Philip P. ed. *Schoolcraft: The Literary Voyageur or Muzzeniegun.* East Lansing, 1962..
McClurken, James M. *Gah-Baeh-Jhagwah-Buk The Way It Happened.* East Lansing, [1991].
Osborn, Chase S. and Stellanova. *Schoolcraft-Longfellow-Hiawatha.* Lancaster, 1942.
Ratigan, William. *Hiawatha and America's Mightest Mile.* Grand Rapids, 1955.
Schoolcraft, Henry Rowe. *Algic Researches...* 2 Vols. New York, 1839.
_____. *The Myth of Hiawatha.* Philadelphia, 1856.
Stedman, Clarence Edmund. *Poets of America.* Cambridge, 1885.
Williams, Mentor L., ed. *Schoolcraft's Indian Legends...* East Lansing, 1991.

Oz at Macatawa

Baum, Frank Joslyn and MacFall, Russel P. *To Please a Child: a Biography of L. Frank Baum...* Chicago, 1961.
Baum, L. Frank. *The Marvelous Land of Oz..* Chicago, 1904.
_____. *Ozma of Oz.* Chicago, 1907.
_____. "To Macatawa," *Grand Rapids Sunday Herald.* 1 Sept. 1907.
Cooke, John Estes [Lyman Frank Baum]. *Tamawaca Folks.* Tamawaca Press, [1907].
Hearn, Michael Patrick, ed. *The Wizard of Oz.* New York, [1983].
Leach, William R. ed. *The Wonderful Wizard of Oz.* Belmont, Ca., [1991].
Mannix, Daniel P. "The Father of the Wizard of Oz," *American Heritage.* Vol. XVI, No. 1 December, 1964. p. 36
Massie, Larry B. *The Holland Area: Warm Friends and Wooden Shoes.* N.P., [1988].
van Reken, Donald. *Macatawa Park: A Chronicle.* Holland, [1991].

Atlantic City of the West

Appleyard, Richard. *Images of the Past.* South Haven, 1984.
Kinney, Troy and Margaret West. *Social Dancing of Today.*

New York, 1914.

Michigan Summer Resorts Including the Michigan East Coast Resorts. 1913 Edition. [Detroit, N.D.].

Norton, Willard, A. *Directory of South Haven, Casco and Covert...* South Haven, 1898.

Residence, Business and Resort Directory of South Haven, Michigan. South Haven, 1902.

Souvenir of the Michigan Peach Belt [Cover title], [Chicago, 1896].

Vargo, George. "South Haven, Ocean Port in Michigan," *Inland Seas.* Vol. 11, No. 1. (Spring, 1955). p. 49.

West Michigan Vacation Directory. N.P. [1927].

Paw Paw Chautauqua

Case, Victoria and Robert O. *We Called it Culture.* New York, 1948.

Farm Journal Illustrated Directory of Van Buren County, Michigan. Philadelphia, 1916.

Harrison, Harry P. and Detzer, Karl. *Culture Under Canvas.* New York, [1958].

Horner, Charles F. *Strike the Tents.* Phildelphia, [1954].

MacLaren, Gay. *Morally We Roll Along.* Boston, 1938.

Paw Paw Chautauqua (promo pamphlets) Paw Paw, 1910, 1911, 1917.

Rowland: *A History of Van Buren County,*

Pigeoners' Lament

Barrows, Walter Bradford. *Michigan Bird Life.* Lansing, 1912.

Case, William L. "Passing of the Passenger Pigeon," *Michigan History Magazine.* Vol. XIV. No. 2. (Spring, 1930), p. 262.

Hartwick, and Tuller: *Oceana County Pioneers.*

Hutchins, Henry Hudson. *Recollections of the Pioneers of Western Allegan County.* [Saugatuck, 1977].

Mershon, William B. *The Passenger Pigeon.* N.Y., 1907.

Cornelian Car

Allegan, Michigan 1838-1963 125th Anniversary Publication. N.P. 1963.

Blood, Howard E. To Shattuck, Dennis: 11 Jan. 1966.

Green, James J. *From Blood-Brothers Machine Company to Rockwell International.* [Allegan], 1978.

Kalamazoo Gazette. 1 Nov. 1914, 25 Nov. 1914.

Massie & Schmitt: *Kalamazoo.*

Joe Pete

"Among the Books," *Michigan History Magazine.* Vol. XIV. Spring No. [1930], p. 356.

Book League Monthly. Vol. II. No. 2. [Dec. 1929]. p. iii.

McClinchey, Florence. *Joe Pete.* New York, 1929.

"Michigan Authors and Their Books," *Michigan Library Bulletin.* March, 1930. p. 106.

Carl Sandburg at Harbert

Detzer, Karl. *Carl Sandburg: A Study in Personality and Background.* New York, (1941).

Kunitz & Haycraft: *Twentieth Century Authors.*

_____. Twenthieth Century Authors. First Supplement. New York, 1955.

Mitzang, Herbert, ed. *The Letters of Carl Sandburg.* New York, (1968).

"Poet's Former Home," *Hometown News, South Bend Tribune.* 2 December 1993. p. 3.

New Books For Old

Allegan County Book Fair. N.P., 1940.

W.K. Kelloggg Foundation: The First Eleven Years 1930-1941. [Chicago], 1942.

The First Twenty-Five Years. W.K. Kelloggg Foundation. N.P. [1955].

Fate of a River

Armstrong, Joe and Pahl, John. *Early Times in Allegan Township.* [Allegan, 1987].

Armstrong & Pahl: *River and Lake.*

History of Allegan & Barry Counties, Michigan.

Warner, Wm. W. "Early History of Michigan," *Michigan Pioneer Collections.* Vol. 27, (1897), p. 289.

INDEX

Born in Grand Rapids, Larry B. Massie grew up in Allegan. Following a tour in Viet Nam as a U.S. Army paratrooper, he worked as a telephone lineman, construction laborer, bartender and in a pickle factory before earning three degrees in history from Western Michigan University. In 1983 he launched a career as a independent historian, specializing in the heritage of the state he loves. He lives with wife and workmate Priscilla and their 35,000 volume library in a rambling old schoolhouse nestled in the Allegan State Forest. Sons Adam, Wallie, Larry Jr. and daughter Maureen insure there is never a dull moment.

Larry and Priscilla Massie's

MICHIGAN HISTORY BOOKS AVAILABLE FROM THE
PRISCILLA PRESS

On the Road to Michigan's Past 288 pages, ill. bib. index. $12.50
Hardbound Limited Edition $18.95

Michigan Memories 288 pages, ill. bib. index. $10.95

Birchbark Belles   310 pages, ill. bib. index. $10.95

Potawatomi Tears and Petticoat Pioneers 296 pages, ill. bib. index.
$10.95

The Romance of Michigan's Past 270 pages, ill. bib. index. $10.95

Pig Boats and River Hogs 296 pages, ill. bib. index. $10.95

Copper Trails and Iron Rails 290 pages, ill. bib. index. $10.95
Hardbound Limited Edition $18.95

Voyages into Michigan's Past 298 pages, ill. bib. index. $10.95

Walnut Pickles and Watermelon Cake: A Century of Michigan
Cookery 354 pages, 8 1/2 x 11, ill. bib. index, hardbound. $24.95

Warm Friends and Wooden Shoes:An Illustrated History of
Holland, Michigan 128 pages, 8 1/2 x 11, ill. bib. index, hardbound.
$19.9

Shipping on individual books $2.00
Two or more books ordered retail—shipping is free
Michigan residents please add 6% sales tax

Order from Priscilla Massie
2109 41ST STREET
ALLEGAN FOREST, MICHIGAN 49010
(616) 673-3633
Please indicate if you would like the author to inscribe the books.